ONE HOPE

BELIEVING GOD WHEN THERE'S EVERY REASON TO
GIVE UP...

MICHAEL MASON

Four Days
Three Words
Two Sisters

One Hope

Believing God when there's every reason to give up...

Michael Mason

Foreword by Jim Henry

Michael Mason Ministries
Hartselle, Alabama

One Hope

Copyright © 2021

First printing June, 2021

Cover design by Abigail Jackson

ISBN: 978-1-953406-22-4 (Paperback)

ISBN: 978-1-953406-23-1 (ebook)

Soncoast Publishing

PO Box 1503

Hartselle, AL 35640

www.soncoastpublishing.com

This book is dedicated to our children…

Alyssa ~ Strong and Determined

Jordan ~ Dependable and Sincere

Garrett ~ Loyal and Genuine

Grayson ~ Authentic and Faithful

Hunter ~ Dedicated and Consistent

These are the daughters we prayed for…
And the sons we always wanted.

ACKNOWLEDGMENTS

I couldn't do what I do without the love of my wife Dawn. She is the answer to many prayers.

I'm thankful for Jim Henry taking the time to write the foreword. He is one of my heroes.

I wouldn't be writing without the encouragement of Evangelist Junior Hill and his wife, Carole. They have loved me like a son.

I am indebted to my parents, Lewis and Ellawee, for their prayers. I'm grateful for my sister, Diana, who has loved me and ministered to me.

Most of all I am thankful to the Lord for His saving grace.

CONTENTS

FOREWORD

~ By Jim Henry ~

Years ago a submarine had mechanical problems and slowly sank to the bottom of the sea. Frantic submariners sought to correct the problem, but the situation seemed hopeless. A diver was able to find the stricken vessel. With no other means to communicate he tapped the hub of the sub letting those inside know, if still alive, that they were aware of their plight. From inside the sub the question came, "Is there any hope?"

Hope is the intangible that drives the inner person. The Apostle Paul included Hope in his trilogy of those things that are eternal: Faith, Hope, Love. As a pastor I've heard it in words, seen it in searching eyes, and felt it in the weight of overwhelming circumstances. I've experienced it in my family. I've seen Hope bring a burst of renewed strength and the rekindling of desire to press on. I've observed the effects of surrender when the spirit swoons and the light goes off.

Hope is usually expressed in one of two ways. One way is to believe that something may happen that's really good, but it's based on happenstance, good luck, or circumstances. Like, "I hope our team wins, but we're a five touchdown underdog." Or, "We hope our son marries that cute girl from church, but he seems to be interested in a gal we don't care for." The Biblical approach is not one of a toss of the dice, but one that is a confident assurance. A line from an old hymn sums up that desired way: "My hope is built on nothing less than Jesus' blood and righteousness."

Michael Mason has taken one of the greatest stories of our Lord's earthly journey and opened up a treasure chest of fresh insights. With accuracy to the Word of God, and with application surrounded by humour and insights into the realities of life he has so keenly observed, you will find easy reading, much encouragement, and above all Hope, focused on the One who alone brings that to the heart ... Jesus Christ.

INTRODUCTION

Hope. It's the one thing everyone wants and few actually have. I've met a few people who have no hope. Many of them were sitting in churches, pretending all was well. What a sad condition – hopeless. Empty. Heart-hurt. Bruised. They've given up on ever being hopeful again. For some, the cancer is back. For others, the marriage is ending. For another, the prodigal child won't come home. Some are still struggling with an addiction. Some are battling depression. Some live in homes with the doors closed and blinds pulled. They live life in isolation. Such is the world in which we live. Much of society has withdrawn to relationships that exist only on a computer screen. We fill our mind with what we read and see in the world and resign ourselves to hopeless lives, hopeless relationships, hopeless religion, and a hopeless future. We don't talk honestly about our need for hope – that would mean admitting we're feeling hopeless. So we smile when we'd rather cry. We laugh to cover the hurt. We continue the charade that all is well, when in reality, we dread the sunrise of another day.

I've often wondered why we don't hear much about hopelessness in church. I'm not suggesting sorrowing should take precedence over celebrating, but I think we overlook reality – the reality of broken hearts and searching souls on every pew. Often we're too busy celebrating someone's happiness to notice another's heartache. For every young lady who's celebrating the birth of a baby, there's another young lady who's lost hope that she will ever be a mother. For every praise report of someone who is finally cancer free, there's another person who fears the worst. For every prodigal that has finally come home, there is another just leaving. I certainly don't want to paint a bleak picture, but I think it is necessary that we see hurting people and be reminded that God sees them too. If you've ever felt hopeless, or even a little hopeless, you know the power of someone's words. May God use us and our words to encourage the hopeless of brighter days ahead.

The question that begs to be asked is simply, "Is there any hope?"

A young mother hopes her malignancy can be treated. A middle-aged man hopes he can overcome his battle with depression. A five-year-old girl at Children's Hospital hopes to run and play again. Everywhere you go and everywhere you look you'll find people searching for hope. They're desperate for a glimmer of possibility that all will soon be well. The possibility that things will improve, that their situation will miraculously change. They're hungry for hope.

I saw this hunger illustrated several years ago. I was privileged to take the trip of a lifetime to Israel, Jordan, and Egypt. While in Jerusalem, we toured the old city and stood with countless others at the Western Wall. What an amazing sight as people from all over the world stood at a wall and prayed. Some were praying for the peace of Israel. Most were uttering prayers I didn't understand and reciting scripture I couldn't read. I felt as if I was on holy ground. Each of us had one thing in common: we longed for hope.

The wall I stood before was as old as most of the Bible. To think about the history of where I stood was humbling. Along with every other person standing there that day, I scribbled a prayer on a scrap of paper and pressed it between the age-old stones that make up the wall. Why did I do that? Did I really believe my prayer pressed between those stones would get the Father's special attention? No. I didn't believe that at all. My hope is in the Lord Jesus. Not in a wall, or in a prayer, or in a place. My hope is in Jesus whose name is above all names. But for a moment I was caught up in the holy-ness of my surroundings. This was a sacred experience for me. I was on holy ground. I felt the presence of a holy God. I was standing where few had stood and feeling what few had felt. What would it hurt to scribble a heart-cry on paper and cram it between the stones? I guess it was another way of expressing the hope I have in God. If it was just another meaningless religious ritual, I trust God will forgive me. We all need a little extra hope.

What about you? What are you hoping for? At night when you can't sleep, what do you think about? What are you praying for? What is it that makes your heart cry? Maybe it's just between you and God. Maybe you've confided in a friend or your husband or wife. Maybe you've lived most of your life with a secret hope. What is it in the depths of your soul that begs for God's attention? I have a friend who hopes her prodigal will soon come home to stay. I know a man who is hoping his wife can be free from depression. I meet so many people who simply say, *"Pray for my son ... pray for my daughter ... pray for my husband ... pray for my wife ...."* and the list goes on. Maybe you've been there, and maybe you're there now. Keep praying for hopeless situations and hopeless people. While medications, doctors, and therapies are often necessary, our only hope in the face of hopelessness is prayer. Don't stop believing. Don't stop hoping.

In this brief book, I want us to go back once again to that time in history when Lazarus died. I want us to feel what the sisters Martha and Mary felt. I want us to join the crowd of weepers as they mourn the death of a friend. I want us to participate in the criticism and speculation about Jesus and wonder aloud, "Why isn't He here?" But more than anything, I want us to experience the hope of Martha and Mary. When everyone thought these women were running to the tomb, they were running to Jesus.

We will re-live four of the longest days ever lived by those who knew and loved Lazarus. Waiting on God is not easy when your need is urgent. Four days can seem like an eternity when you needed Him four days ago.

We will hear again three of the most wonderful words ever spoken. When Jesus said, *"Lazarus, come forth,"* the crowd that day couldn't believe their eyes, the whole world changed, and the devil had a heart attack.

We will look once again at the lives of two of the Bible's most amazing women - Martha and Mary. We'll learn something about them, but we'll learn more about ourselves.

And finally, we'll be reminded of the One Hope in all the world that changes people and their circumstances. This hope has a name. Jesus.

FOUR DAYS

Even when Jesus is late ... He's worth the wait.

John 11:1-6

I find it interesting to read statistics about the amount of time people spend doing certain things. Like how much of our life we spend sleeping, driving, texting, and waiting. A Timex survey reveals that Americans wait on average of 20 minutes a day for the bus or train, 32 minutes whenever they visit a doctor, and 28 minutes waiting in security lines whenever they travel. On the average, Americans wait 21 minutes for their spouse to get ready to go out (reference.com). Evidently, we're all waiting on someone or something.

I've waited in line more than I want to think about. On my first trip to Disney I waited in line for over an hour to ride Dumbo, which I had already timed as I watched about 200 people ahead of me. Dumbo lasted all of 49 seconds. Alyssa loved it, and I loved her, so I waited.

Throughout their life, the average person spends five years waiting in lines, and six months of that is waiting at traffic lights (thefactsite.com). Waiting…For…The… Light…To…Change. What do we do while we're waiting? Check our phone. Change the music. Read a book. Write a book. Life is filled with waiting.

I've waited at restaurants longer than any sane person ought to wait. Is the Outback Steakhouse really worth a one-hour wait on Saturday night? No. But that "Blooming Onion" is pretty good. You've been there. You've got your name on the list. The girl at the front desk has said your wait will only be twenty minutes or so. And then your twenty minutes has turned into forty minutes. Forty minutes turns into what feels like two weeks. Everyone else's buzzer is buzzing. People who arrived much later than you are going in. They're laughing. They're eating steaks, hot rolls, salads, and drinking ice tea. And you're left waiting outside with a bucket of peanuts.

I have waited for my children to come home. It's a Saturday night and they're already forty minutes late. About that time they pull into the driveway. They lost track of time. Their phone died. They got caught in traffic. They had to stop for gas. They forgot. They were abducted by aliens. It's on those nights when I have to mentally go back in time and remember when I prayed for God to bless us with children. Don't get me wrong. I love them, but on those nights I was in no mood to throw a welcome home party. I was tired and I was tired of waiting. Can I get a witness?

Brad Paisley, one of my favorite country music singers, had it right when he sang about *"Waitin' On A Woman."* I've waited for Dawn a few times. And she's waited on me some, too. Whether it's hair, nails, or shopping for that perfect dress, I can tell you here and now, some things are worth the wait. I don't mind waiting on Mrs. Dawny. It's like a friend of mine who was accused of being hen-pecked. He replied, *"It's not so bad, especially when you love the hen that's doing the pecking."*

I have waited on my mother and dad at the doctor. Most of the waiting I ever did for my mother was at places where the word "cardiac" was on the letterhead. Mother had her first heart attack when she was only fifty-six. She lived the last seventeen years of her life visiting doctors on a regular basis and waiting in waiting rooms and doing all she could to live as long as she could. I was happy to wait with her. And after her passing I did some waiting with my dad. He passed away at the age of 89, having lived 14 years after Mother's passing. The last five years of his life he struggled with dementia. I am grateful for a mom and dad who waited on me. The least I could do was wait with them. As the years quickly pass I am realizing more and more the value of the time I spent with my parents. Those doctor appointments were not interruptions. They were opportunities to spend most of a day with people I loved more than words can express. My dad and I waited on Mother. I waited with him. We've waited for good news, and we've waited for bad news. But more than anything, we waited together. And because of who I was waiting on and waiting with, the time was well spent.

One night several years ago in Louisville, Kentucky, I waited about an hour for firemen to come and pull me out of an elevator that refused to cooperate. I was at Southern Seminary in an old building in a small elevator going from the first to the third floor in the middle of a thunderstorm. One strong bolt of lightning and a clap of thunder and the world's next greatest preacher was stuck in an elevator. I should have taken the stairs, but there I was, alone in what felt like an oversized microwave oven. My cell phone wasn't connecting so I yelled for help a few times with no response from the other side. I opened that little door in the elevator that is marked "phone" and expected to find a bundle of wires like you see in most elevators. But this one actually had a phone that worked. The guy who answered laughed. I'm not joking. My life is in jeopardy, and the fella working the phones at the seminary office that night thought my situation was funny. I didn't think it was funny, and the fireman who finally opened up the top of the elevator didn't think it was funny either. Especially when he began to pull me up through a hole about the size of a laptop.

I heard a story about three men years ago in a maternity waiting room, when men actually waited for their wives to give birth. The nurse came out and said to the first man, "Congratulations, your wife has just given birth to twins." He stood up and with a big grin on his face said, "Isn't that amazing, I play baseball for the Minnesota Twins." The nurse came out again a few minutes later and said to the second fellow, "Congratulations, your wife has just given birth to triplets." He stood up and almost laughed saying, "Isn't that amazing, I work for the 3M Company." Just then the third man jumped up, grabbed his coat and hat and headed for the door. The nurse asked, "Sir, where are you going?" He said, "Somewhere to lay down. I work for Seven-Up."

I have waited for my children to be born. I have waited for my car to be repaired. I have waited for my name to be called. I have waited at water parks, ball parks, theme parks, and amusement parks. I have waited to take tests. I have waited for church to start. I have waited to buy tickets. I have waited at restaurants. I have waited at Wal-Mart, K-Mart, and any other "Mart" you can name. I have waited on the line, and I have waited in line. I have even waited to be waited on.

And I have waited on God. And I guess there have been a number of times when God has waited on me. Waiting on God is not only difficult, it can also be an adventure. Because you never know exactly how He will answer a prayer or how He will direct your life. Most of us are waiting on God for something. Waiting for a better job, waiting for the kids to grow up, waiting for a bigger paycheck, a nicer home, retirement, etc. But honestly, I know many people who are waiting for their life to get better. They just want to enjoy life. After waiting a while for a short list of improvements in my life, I determined to enjoy what I had. Sometimes, even though your world isn't perfect, if you'll look around it's far better than the life some folks are living. Sometimes we need to thank God for what we have instead of waiting for what we don't have. Sometimes we need to focus on what we want instead of what we don't want. A shift in focus can change everything.

Dawn and I have waited through dark days and bad news, believing God and trusting Him for the miraculous. We continued to wait and believe even when faced with the hard realities of death and divorce. In 2010, her husband at the time was diagnosed with ALS. About a year later, in 2011, I received the bad news that my marriage was ending. While it is tempting to suggest one was worse than the other or just as bad, we have learned that heartache is not a competition. The only difference between major and minor surgery is whether or not it's happening to you.

Dawn's waiting involved doctor appointments, hospitalizations, medications, and a long list of other ups and downs that required patience. Her waiting included loving her husband unconditionally and believing God for a miracle. My waiting involved quiet uncertainties, two steps forward and three steps back, separation, and the distance only those who have reluctantly participated in divorce would understand.

But it was in the waiting that we found grace we didn't know existed.

It was in the waiting that we experienced a shifted focus off of our losses and toward our blessings.

It was in the waiting for a miracle that Dawn experienced the miracle of peace greater than her pain.

It was in the waiting that I found the miracle of grace greater than my grief.
It was in the waiting that our faith in God grew.

It was in the waiting that the scriptures leaped off the page, alive with meaning.

It was in the waiting that we found God to be bigger than we had ever known.

Shadrach, Meshach, and Abednego didn't choose the fire they were thrown into. They simply refused to bow and suddenly found themselves bound for a fiery furnace. Surely those three men in the fire were pleasantly shocked as well. God didn't put out the fire. Instead, it was His very presence that protected them. Dawn and I were in the fire of another kind. A fire we would have never chosen. A storm we would have never predicted. A hurt that could either ruin our faith or reshape it. God didn't put out our fires, either. But just as with those three Hebrew men, it was the undeniable presence of the Lord Himself that sustained us. We weren't alone in the fire.

Dawn and I waited when we wanted to give up. We held on when it would have been easy to let go. In fact, we found ourselves unusually strong in the storm. I imagine many of you reading this can relate. You're not alone. Churches are filled with people that believed when it would have been easier to quit. In the hardship, in the storm, all you've ever believed will be tested and tried. You only thought you knew about grace till you actually depended on it. After that, singing *Amazing Grace* will never be the same.

Think about Martha and Mary. They waited four days. Four days of frustration. Four days of anxiety and anticipation. Four days of faith-testing and faith-stretching patience and impatience. Martha and Mary felt every emotion one can imagine during those four days. Most of us have been in similar situations when we've waited and prayed and prayed and waited and waited and prayed some more. But it's the uncertainty of the outcome that drives us to the greater certainty of hope...hope in Christ.

We've been there when a loved one has died and gone on to be with the Lord. We had waited, hoped, and prayed that all would be well. We had prayed the cancer would be healed, that the surgery would go well, that the medicine would work, and that the doctors would find a cure. And we've been there when they didn't. Our loved one passed away. And we're left holding only to what we've believed. And during those times it is often *what* we believe that holds us, keeps us, and steadies us.

Even though my mother's death was sudden, I had been waiting on it since her first heart attack seventeen years earlier. She was weak and became weaker. The doctor said she could come home the next morning. So on a Friday night when I visited her, I didn't stay long. She seemed happy and said she felt fine. I stayed in Mother's room just a few brief minutes and promised her I'd see her next morning. My, how I wish I had not been in such a rush. I have replayed that night in her hospital room over and over again in my mind. We simply never know when we will have that last visit. That's why we should make every visit meaningful.

My dad was suffering in his last few weeks of life. Dementia had taken its toll and we were praying for Dad to pass peacefully. What a wonderful and happy man he was. At his funeral service I spoke about how he had taught us to live, laugh, and love. But in those last weeks and days, we knew his living was over. My sister and I were at his bedside the morning he passed. I had just leaned over and said to him, *"Daddy, we're both here. We love you. If you want to rest, you can. We understand…"* About a minute later he took two deep breaths and stepped out of this life and into eternity. It was the most peaceful thing I've ever witnessed. He had hope beyond the grave. His was not a hopeless passing. Now, knowing where my mom and dad are makes Heaven even more inviting.

In John chapter eleven, the funeral is over. Martha and Mary are facing reality, and they begin to wonder about what if…? "What if Jesus had been here? What if Jesus had not gone out of town? What if we had gotten word to Him sooner? What if…"

The "what-ifs" we ask during times of sickness and dying are like a self-imposed therapy that helps us deal with the ultimate reality of "what-now?" In light of that, let's ask the same question Martha and Mary must have asked. "What *if* Jesus had been there? What if Jesus had simply been there to touch Lazarus' body, to speak words of life, to do something – anything?" They must have thought, "If Jesus had been here we wouldn't be in this situation and Lazarus wouldn't be in the grave." The truth is, the presence of Jesus *does* make all the difference.

But the other truth is, Lazarus died. He stopped breathing. He was wrapped in grave clothes and buried. And so someone might ask, "If Jesus really cares, then why did He leave town about the time Lazarus died?" Good question. God has never worked according to our schedule. According to our timing, the Lord is sometimes late or doesn't come at all. Yet nothing surprises God. He has a perfect plan about every event in our lives. We may live ten or twenty years before we can look back and clearly see the hand of God in tragedies and heartaches. Consider it one of the great mysteries as to why Jesus left when He did. In John 11:4 we read Jesus' words, *"This sickness is not unto death, but for the glory of God, that the Son of God may be glorified through it."* Yet Martha's concern rings loud and clear, *"Lord, if you had been here my brother would not have died…"* In hindsight we see how God used it all for His glory. But in real time it is a mystery we share with Martha, *"Lord if you had been here…"*

I don't know who said it but I agree with it, *"We may set our sails, but God controls the wind."* Think about those words. And yes, I believe God controls the winds of blessing as well as adversity. And while I believe He is sovereign in what He does, I often don't understand why He does what He does. I've tried to fully comprehend, only to exhaust myself mentally and emotionally. As a believer I've learned to wait on God to fill my sails with the winds of the Holy Spirit and take me to the places that are pleasing to Him. I can wish and I can wonder. But the absolute best thing I can do is believe and wait. In God's perfect timing He will show me why He didn't answer my prayers in the way I had thought He would.

And so Martha and Mary, if the "what-ifs" become the "what-nows," what do we do now? There is only one thing to do. Wait on Jesus.

Over the past several years we have watched television coverage as family members gathered at churches in coal mining communities waiting, watching, and praying that their loved ones would walk out of a collapsed mine. We cried when they did and cried when they didn't. We wondered aloud what we would do if we were in that situation. We also watched family members grieve over their baby girl who had fallen and was trapped in an abandoned well. We stayed up late glued to the TV praying she would be rescued and soon resting in her mother's arms. We also watched as a submarine, hundreds of feet below the surface, is unable to restart its engines. We hurt with the family and prayed for those on board. In those few brief hours we felt a kinship to those grieving families who waited anxiously to hear the fate of their loved ones. And then finally, we watched as all those on board were met with applause and tears. It was nothing short of a miracle.

When Lazarus came out of the grave, it was nothing short of a miracle. He had been dead four days. He was wrapped in grave cloths and the tomb was sealed. The funeral was over. It was a done deal. ***Then Jesus came....*** Think with me for a minute about three possible scenarios.

You've waited in the waiting room more times than you can count. You've slept in an uncomfortable chair in an awkward position all night long just to be near your loved one. You've waited to hear from the doctor. You've waited to see your husband or wife or child or mom or dad for what could be the last time. Your body is tired and your eyes are heavy. You've worked all day and stayed up all night. You've eaten little, slept even less, and cried a lot. You'd like to shower at home and be in your own bed for one night, but you can't bear the thought of your loved one dying without you there. All you can do is wait.

You've waited past midnight too many times for your son or daughter to come home. Your mind has raced up and down the highways in fear that she was involved in a wreck or that his car had been found abandoned on the side of some dark back road, and you'd be getting a call any minute. It's not so much your son or daughter you're worried about. You've taught them well.

You're worried about the guy driving the other car. The guy who's had too much to drink. The guy who's too high to drive. You can only imagine what could have happened. Why is he so late? Where could she be? Why won't they answer their phone?

You've waited for your marriage to get better. You believed there were brighter days ahead. You've prayed for him. You've prayed for her. You've fussed and fought and thought about packing and leaving in the middle of the night. Neither one wants to talk about it. He's critical and overbearing. She's possessive and domineering. If one or both of you doesn't change, the marriage is over. What will happen to the kids? Where will you live? The questions, confusion, and chaos continue to mount. Sometimes you have felt that the Devil had painted a bullseye on your marriage and was using your home for target practice. What can you do? Who do you turn to? Does God even know what you're going through? Sometimes it's hard to wait.

Martha and Mary asked the obvious, "Where have you been?" Had Jesus been there, everything would have been different. But He wasn't. We've all had days like that. Days when we believed and prayed and trusted, but we wondered why God didn't show up and do something miraculous. Days when we felt alone. Days when all...we...had...was...hope. And I can hear that pastor just now, "Just because Jesus is in the boat doesn't mean you'll avoid the storm." And I agree. But having Jesus in your boat sure beats facing the storm alone. And then there are some folks that believe if Jesus is in your boat you will never face stormy weather. They believe if Jesus is Lord as He should be in your life, then you will be healed, you will have wealth, and all your dreams will come true.

I wish that were true. But it is not. Not only should you ask Peter, you should also ask the Apostle Paul. He had some sort of *"thorn in the flesh."* We really have no idea what his thorn was. What we know is God didn't remove it. He was called, maybe even compelled, to live with it. Just because Jesus is Lord of your life doesn't mean He'll remove the thorns in your flesh. Waiting on God and dealing with thorns can be emotionally demanding.

He allowed them to run out of wine at a wedding party, and then He turned the water in to wine. He allowed them to need food on a hillside, and then He blessed five loaves and two fishes and fed thousands. He allowed Lazarus to die, and then went back and raised him to life. If your situation appears hopeless, you're not alone. Don't give up. Martha and Mary were not without hope. They had absolute confidence that had Jesus been there Lazarus would still be alive. And we can have that same hope.

FOUR DAYS: John 11:17-22

Pain is the same color whether you are saved or lost. Pain feels the same whether you're rich or poor, a college graduate or high school dropout, a stockbroker in New York or a cotton-farmer in Alabama. Pain is painful regardless of who you are. Martha and Mary had felt the pain of losing a loved one for several days. Lazarus had been sick and dying. Now he was dead and buried. They felt what we feel, and maybe even greater because Jesus was not there when He could have been.

Think for a minute about that statement, "Jesus was not there." Think about *Jesus*. **Jesus** was not there. He was able to restore sight to the blind, speech to the dumb, hearing to the deaf, and He could erase the leper's spots. It would not have been as big a deal if Peter or James or John was not there. But we're talking about Jesus. When Jesus is not where you had hoped He'd be, there is an obvious absence. Other people were there. A large number of friends were there. But the one person they needed at that one moment in their lives was not there.

Think about that statement again, "Jesus was not there." Concentrate on the word, *not*. Jesus was **not** there. We like to preach proudly that God is with us, and there's nothing He cannot do. Friend, I believe there are some things God chooses not to do. There are some places He chooses not to be. There are some folks He chooses not to heal. On this day in scripture He chose not to be there when Lazarus died. My wife Dawn was married to Arvid for a number of years. She was there throughout his diagnosis, sickness, and eventual death due to ALS. She can relate to Martha and Mary. Dawn says, *"God doesn't waste anything."* There is a comfort for the believer in those words. But for the unbeliever or the agnostic, that kind of faith is insanity. However, for Dawn and for Arvid, they believed whether in life or in death God was good and could even use ALS for good. He doesn't waste anything. In the story of Lazarus, all the intricate details that created fear, worry, anxiety, and questions were used for their good and His glory. If you're facing a Lazarus event in your life, look for God on the dark days, listen for God in the uncertainty, and believe God when it'd be easier to give up. He doesn't waste anything.

Think once more about that statement, "Jesus was not there." Think about the word *there*. Jesus was not **there**. We like to think God is on our side. As Americans, we like to think that God is either Republican or Democrat. As Baptists or Methodists or Catholics we like to think that He is one of us. People have tried for years to put God in a neatly wrapped package. He's been white, Black, Hispanic, racist.... He's been pro-life, and He's been pro-choice. The bad news for all of us with a God-box is that He won't fit in our box. He's bigger than the box. He's bigger than our theology. He's bigger than our political agenda. He's bigger than you. He's bigger than me. *Just because Jesus isn't where we think He should be, He is always where He needs to be.* And rest assured He is always doing His Father's business.

Day 1: John 11:3

The message is delivered. Lazarus dies...

Someone might have shouted, get help! This was urgent. This was desperation. Go tell Jesus that Lazarus is sick! Jesus was at Bethabara, about twenty miles from Bethany. The messenger soon arrived with the sad news that Lazarus was sick. But, Jesus sent him back the next day with the words recorded in John 11:4. *"This sickness is not unto death, but for the glory of God."* Then Jesus waited two more days before He left for Bethany, and by the time He and His disciples arrived, Lazarus had been dead four days. This means Lazarus had died the very day the messenger left to tell Jesus!

Jesus could have given in to His own personal desires as well as the wishes of those who sent for Him. He could have left immediately, traveled back to Bethany and healed Lazarus from his sickness. He could have and He would have, but He was doing something bigger. The Bible is clear that Jesus loved Lazarus. The easy thing to do was go back and heal him. The difficult thing to do was wait on the Father's will.

I am learning to wait on the Father's will. After almost forty years of ministry the waiting hasn't become any easier; it has only become more necessary. Waiting for the will of God has always been necessary, but growing older has helped me understand that. In my mental rearview mirror, I see a few times I should have waited on the Father's will. But I was in a hurry. I had all the answers. I was zealous. I was also strong-willed. My dad warned me when I was younger about going off *"half-cocked."* It means to act on impulse or to make decisions irrationally. That saying is derived from the operation of an older type of firearm. If a gun was only half-cocked it was not ready to fire. Dad's advice rings loud and clear. Wait on the Lord. Wait on the

Father's will. Give God room to work in your life. Allow Him time and space to orchestrate His will. Don't go off half-cocked.

We seldom think of Jesus waiting for the Father's approval on what He would do next and where He would go. But Jesus waited, in some ways, just like we do. Everywhere He went and in everything He did He was following His Father's direction. And in the background He could hear the cross calling His name. But for most of those thirty-three years the time was not right. Jesus was waiting for the Father to lead Him.

Day 2: John 11:11

The messenger returns to Bethany. Lazarus' body is buried. Jesus is still in Bethabara...

Someone might have shouted, give up! With all the critics in the crowds that day, someone surely took the opportunity to take a shot at Jesus. Give up, they must have cried. He's not coming back. He doesn't care. Some of those whose hearts were broken because of Lazarus' death may have believed the critics. Some may have believed the rumors as to why Jesus was not back in town by now. Chances are, some of you reading this know a little about rumors. Once a rumor is started, it's hard to stop. And, regardless of how ridiculous the rumor, some will believe it. A rumor about a famous politician or athlete is bad enough. But when the rumoring creeps its way into the church and among believers, the end result is nothing short of tragic. Innocent people get caught in the crossfire. Good men and women are hurt. And some are destroyed. Rumoring is not new. It's as old as the Bible.

The messenger returned to Bethany soon after delivering the bad news. But he returned to town without Jesus. Jesus stayed behind. If a picture paints a thousand words, then this picture paints a million. The messenger was sent to tell Jesus about Lazarus. And even though the expectation of Jesus' return is not specifically spelled out in scripture, the idea that He would return immediately is certainly implied.

So, get the picture. A lone messenger re-enters Bethany. Some of the friends and family run to meet him. You can see the distress on their faces. Some are confused. Some are upset. Some are weeping. Some can't believe their ears. Now all those rumors begin to make sense. Where is Jesus? I thought He and Lazarus were close friends? What could possibly be more important than Lazarus? Is He even coming? And so the chatter begins. Lazarus is dead, and it appears Jesus is not coming back for the funeral.

I remember well a conversation I had with a man who had grown to believe God didn't care about him anymore. This man was very comfortable financially, had a beautiful family, and was well respected in the community. But in the privacy of my office, he confided just how miserable he was. The money was good, but it didn't make him happy. The wife was a wonderful lady, but they seldom talked even when they sat together in the living room of their home. And even though he was well respected by others, he talked as if his entire life was a lie. As his pastor I did my best to encourage him by saying, *"I want you to know I care about you, but more than anything God cares about you. He knows just where you are and what you're facing."* At that point he thanked me for caring but said that he believed *God* didn't really care about him at all.

I suppose the world is full of folks like that man. They have everything to make them happy, but they're miserable. Their hope has been in building a resume, accumulating wealth, reaching milestones in their career, and establishing a name for themselves. But they've never really cared about God, and now they feel as if God doesn't care about them. Friend, if you will seek the Lord, you will find Him. And you will find that He cares. God cared about Martha and Mary, and He cares about you.

The question that begs to be asked is, "Why didn't Jesus come back immediately?" Based on my vast amounts of theological training and education my answer is simply, "I don't know." I wish I could impress you with opinions and ideas as to what Jesus was doing and what was so important in Bethabara that He couldn't break away and come home to Martha and Mary. But the fact remains, we simply do not know.

"I don't know" has become one of my favorite answers to life's questions. There was a time, well over twenty years ago, when I felt obligated to give an answer to every question asked regarding the Bible. After almost forty years in the ministry I finally feel free enough to say, "I don't know." First of all, it's the truth. And second, what a wonderful reality that there are some questions we can't answer on this side of eternity. We don't always have a neat package to deliver to skeptics and critics. We know the death of Lazarus was for the glory of God. But other than that, we have no idea why Jesus waited while the family wept. Never be afraid to say, "I don't know." Your answer will be a means of worship. God is so big that there are some questions that cannot be answered.

Even though we don't know why Jesus stayed behind and sent the messenger back alone, let's use our imagination to understand what we know Jesus was *not* doing. He was not just killing time. He was not wasting the day with idle chit-chat among the locals. What we know about Him at other times when we see Him in scripture is clear: He was always on a mission. He was feeding hungry people or healing sick people or loving hated people or saving lost people. That's what Jesus did and chances are, that's what He was doing while in Bethabara. Don't even think He was doing nothing. I believe He was anxiously awaiting the Father's permission to go back and call forth Lazarus from the dead. I believe He could hardly wait for the resurrection of Lazarus. Imagine that.

Day 3: John 11:31

Waiting and weeping. Jesus is still in Bethabara. He waits another day then returns to Bethany...

Someone in the crowd might have shouted, "Get over it! Get over it, and let's get back to the way it was before Jesus ever came to our town. Go back to the way things were before Jesus came supposing to be our Savior. Lazarus is dead. Let's get on with whatever is next." I have a hard time imagining life without Jesus. Life without hope. But I am also aware that most of the world lives life without Jesus. And in a nation like the United States, there are many who would silence the church if given the opportunity. What would life look like without Jesus? What would our world look like without the influence of Jesus-loving Christians? Since I'm writing a book about hope, I would have to say a world without Jesus would be absolutely hopeless.

Imagine the scenario: Friends and acquaintances join in the weeping, as Jewish people in that day were accustomed to do. The idea of weeping here is not a gentle shedding of tears. This is described by some as, *"a loud weeping...a lamentation."*

Some of those folks who came to the funeral of Lazarus were professional weepers. They weren't there to offer hope or help. They were there for one reason. They were there to weep. But there were also sincere, broken-hearted people who came. Lazarus had been their friend. And they wept, too. And many wept without hope.

In rural Alabama people still come to the home of the person who has just died. But they're not there to weep. They've come to bring food. They come in large numbers and most of them bring a bucket or bag or box of fried chicken. Whether it's Colonel Sanders, Popeyes, Wal-Mart, Zaxby's, Chick-Fil-A, or Publix, fried chicken is still the go-to food for grieving families in north Alabama. Those folks who show up bearing the nuggets and wings and such shortly after the passing of a loved one are some of the best people on the face of the earth. They love the Lord, and they love the grieving family, and they love fried chicken. Not only will they bring enough for your family. If you ask, they'll stay and help you eat it. Good people. Good chicken.

I have read that when a Jewish person died in the days of Jesus, the body was prepared for burial and was placed in the grave immediately after death. It was customary to bury the body within twenty-four hours after the person passed away. The body was bound hand and foot with grave clothes, and the face was wrapped with a cloth. The Jewish burial practice was to wash the body, anoint it with perfumes, and then bind the hands and feet, as well as the jaw. Afterwards, the family would sit in their house and mourn, visiting with friends and neighbors for a week.

We've been there. Whether it's at a home or a funeral home, we've sat with the family. We've wept. We've remembered. We've wished there'd been more time. We've talked about "Lazarus" and how much better off he is than we are. Day three is not easy. Reality for Martha and Mary begins to set in. Lazarus is dead, and Jesus isn't coming back any time soon. Lazarus may be better off, but the family seems to be getting worse. Surely they were asking, "Where is Jesus when we need Him the most?"

I've been to more funerals and funeral homes than most people. Going to those places and praying with grieving families is a part of my job. But just because it's a part of my job, it doesn't mean I enjoy it. Some days I have dreaded it. Don't get me wrong—I love the people and I care about the families left behind. My dread is in regard to those families that have no hope, no faith in God, and have no interest or intention of getting right with God before *they* die. The deceased person doesn't bother me. But the living family members weeping without hope as well as rejecting their only Hope really burdens me. I realize I have a great opportunity to present the Gospel of Christ, but I also realize the sad reality that many don't and won't believe.

Then there are those folks who say things like, *"Don't cry."* I've always thought that was an odd thing to say to people at a funeral. Crying at the loss of a loved one is a natural thing to do. They not only say, *"Don't cry,"* but they also try to comfort the family by saying, *"He's in a better place."* Or, *"He looks so natural."* Friend, go ahead and cry. Jesus wept at the death of Lazarus for a number of reasons. And regardless of His reasons for weeping, if Jesus can cry at a funeral you can, too. And they may be right. He *is* in a better place, but we're not. So go ahead and weep. As a believer, you can weep for joy at the promise of Heaven.

Day 4: John 11:30-43

Jesus comes home. Lazarus is raised...

Someone might have shouted, "Get ready!" For all the doubters and critics and skeptics, there had to be at least one believer. One believer who might have shouted, "Get ready. Help is on the way!" What a few miserable days they had been through. What a season of grieving and gut-wrenching agony they had experienced. What a time they must have had with all the weepers weeping without hope. But all that was about to change. Jesus was coming home. Lazarus was about to be awakened from his sleep.

Look at John 11:43. *"Now when He had said these things, He cried with a loud voice, 'Lazarus, come forth!'"* This was not a suggestion by

Jesus. This was a command. Jesus cried with a loud voice, *"Lazarus, come forth!"* The great evangelist of the nineteenth century, D. L. Moody said, *"Jesus had to call Lazarus by name because if he hadn't, everybody in the grave would have come forth!"* Imagine that. All of death, Hell, and the grave trembled. Some of the fires in Hell must have smoldered just a little. All of Heaven rejoiced. Lazarus was jerked from the hands of the grave and pulled back to life on earth. What a testimony to the greatness of God and the goodness of His mercies.

Most of us have had our own personal version of day one, day two, and day three. And thank God many of us have known the joy of day four. On day four the healing came. On day four they finally came home from the hospital. Day four was when they went back to work. They enjoyed their family and friends. Their marriage was restored. The addict was delivered. The alcoholic was healed. The wayward child came home. Day four is a miracle. Day four is what we've prayed for.

I mentioned earlier about the passing of my father. It was a bittersweet *day four*. Dad didn't come home. He went to Heaven. He didn't get out of the bed and walk and talk like he had in younger years. He quietly stepped out of this world and into the presence of the Lord. Some would say what happened to my dad was unanswered prayer. And they would be wrong. My dad lived on earth 89 years. 85 of those years he was healthy and strong. We prayed that he would die. It was a difficult prayer to pray. I watched my dad suffer with dementia and go from robust and happy to weak and frail, not knowing where he was or who I was. His healing came in Heaven. He was suddenly absent from the body and present with the Lord. Day four was a good day indeed.

Just because Jesus was out of Town didn't mean He was out of Touch.

I want to go back and visit the question we asked earlier. Why did Jesus wait two days in Bethabara? And what was He doing? Again, we really don't know. We believe He was waiting for the Heavenly Father to send Him back to raise Lazarus to life. Don't you think Jesus *wanted* to be in Bethany? Don't you think He *wanted* to go back right then and raise Lazarus from the dead? Lazarus died soon after the messenger left to deliver the message, and had Jesus begun the journey to Bethany at that very moment, Lazarus would have still died. Jesus stayed away through four days of death and dying. His heart may have been in Bethany, but the will of God for Him was to be in Bethabara.

Why did He wait? The message was sent, *"Lazarus is sick,"* but Jesus already knew. He had divine knowledge of his death. In John 11:14 He said, *"Lazarus is dead."* And in 11:42 He prayed for Lazarus' resurrection that others *"…may believe you have sent me."* And in 11:4 He said plainly, *"This sickness is not unto death, but for the glory of God, that the Son of God may be glorified through it."*

Bethany is only a short distance from Jerusalem, which was the place where Jesus would suffer and die. Jesus knew that Lazarus' death, burial, and resurrection was a glimpse of His own. Jesus waited until all hope was gone. At a time that seemed to be much too late, Jesus came and resurrected Lazarus. To God be the glory! Lazarus is alive! And Jesus is Lord!

I love the idea that God is never late. He's never caught in traffic. He'll never have a meeting that lasts longer than expected. He'll never be caught by surprise or have to cancel an appointment. He is always the same. His grace is always sufficient.

As we think about Martha and Mary and their long, drawn out, four-day ordeal, they could never have imagined how this tragedy would turn out. If they had been writing this story, they could have never predicted the ending. Lazarus walking out of the grave was unbelievable. Finally, Jesus was back in town and once again Lazarus was alive. Their miracle was worth the wait.

Waiting on God...

There are at least two other passages in scripture that show us the perfect timing of God. If you think God is running about four days late, think again. In Daniel 6:16-22 Daniel was in the lion's den waiting for God to provide a way out. The king's decree was established. Daniel could have lost his life, but instead the lions lost their appetite. God could have prevented Daniel's jail time in the lion's den. God could have stirred the king's heart earlier. God could have proven the integrity of Daniel in a number of other less life-threatening ways. But He didn't. He waited until Daniel was actually in the den of lions before He intervened.

I like to think that Daniel slept that night right between two of those lions. The very thing that was meant to destroy him, God would have used to protect him if necessary. God had Daniel right where He wanted him, safe and secure in a den full of lions. The den of lions did not make Daniel the man he was, it only revealed the man he was. Calloused knees and a courageous spirit marked him long before the lion's den identified him. His death sentence only proved his faithfulness.

In Daniel 3:15-26, Shadrach, Meshach, and Abednego were in the fiery furnace waiting for God to send the fourth man. They had confidence that God would save them, but if not they would trust Him anyway. Don't you envy, just a little, the confidence of these three Hebrew men? Don't get me wrong, I'm not volunteering to be tossed into the fiery furnace; but if I was thrown in, I can only hope I would have the courage to be as confident as they were.

Why did it have to come to this? A fiery furnace? Did God really have to allow things to get to this point? Couldn't

Nebuchadnezzar have learned his lesson another way? Was it necessary to put the lives of those Hebrew men in jeopardy? What amazing truths we can learn from these men. God will be with us in the midst of the fire. Just trust Him even when faith doesn't make sense. Something was happening in the furnace. And something was happening in Lazarus' tomb. Be patient. There's a fourth man in the fire, and there's a Savior on His way home. Don't give up.

Four days... Days one, two, and three are pretty common. Very seldom do you hear of a day four - a day when a life is changed. Days one, two, and three never make the headlines. People quit and give up on God on days one, two, and three. Folks stop believing in the power of prayer on days one, two, and three.

But on the fourth day everything changes.

2

THREE WORDS

When Jesus speaks, everything changes.

John 11:43

Three words can change your life. Just ask Lazarus.

Really, you can say a lot with just three words. For instance, if I walked through the door this afternoon and said to Dawn, "I'm craving sushi," I'm pretty sure she would call and schedule a doctor appointment for me. I have friends that tell me I don't know what I'm missing. But I guarantee you this, I'm not eating my fish, steak, or chicken raw. So I've got three words for you if you want to know how I like my sushi: fried, baked, or grilled. Thank you.

Imagine saying words like, "I love you." "Let's get married." "Honey, guess what?" "It's a girl." "It's a boy." Three simple words can <u>change</u> your life. Three words spoken by Jesus brought Lazarus <u>back</u> to life.

Oh, the power of three words. My life has been changed over the past several years as a result of three words. Words like, "I barely graduated," "the real world," "get a job," "go to college," "I got saved," "I'm getting married," "having a baby," "having another baby," "going to seminary," "buying a house," "buying another house," "Mother is sick," "Mother passed away," "pastoring a church," "traveling and preaching," "things are tough," "filing for divorce," "Dad has dementia," "I don't understand," "God is good," "grace is sufficient," "I'm not quitting," "lunch with Dawn," "dinner with Dawn," "I'm marrying Dawn," "merging our families," "blessed beyond measure…"

I could go on with all the words that changed my life, but the greatest three life-changing words I ever uttered went something like this, *"Lord, save me."* That was in 1982. I had returned from a youth camp where I had gone to meet girls but wound up meeting God. The name of the place is Camp Sumatanga near Gadsden, Alabama. That camp will always be special to me. God moved in my life that week, and when I returned home God was still after me. Late one evening after getting out of night classes at the junior college, I drove alone through Decatur, Alabama to what the locals know as the Point Mallard Prayer Chapel. I was so hungry for God and searching for His will. I was eagerly listening, believing that God was speaking to my heart. That evening in that prayer chapel, just me and God had a meeting that changed my life. There was no special music…no one preached…but the Holy Spirit sure worked me over. That's been almost forty years ago, but I remember it as if it was last night.

After about thirty minutes of wrestling with God, I prayed something like this: *"Lord, if this is You, and if this is real, I want all You have for me. Save me."* I am so glad to tell you all these years later it was Him, and it was real, and it still is. Let me clearly state - Jesus Christ came into my heart and changed my life. I have never been the same. He forgave all my sin. He made me His own. All because of His great love and my willingness to pray, *"Lord, save me."*

Those words from me to the Lord were not an ending, but a beginning of a life I would live for Him. It was not long after that night at the prayer chapel that I answered God's call on my life to preach. I have written down a brief narrative of what happened, but I also relive that night in my memory from time to time. I remember the damp evening air. It was about ten at night, and I remember the quietness. I remember the rough bench I was sitting on. I remember chill bumps even though it was late spring. I remember looking around to see if anyone else was there. I knew He was with me. I sensed His presence. The chill I felt was the undeniable presence of God. I remember tears in my eyes. I remember talking to Him as if He was seated right beside me. I remember I didn't see lightning or hear thunder, but I knew my life was changed. He saved me.

WONDERFUL WORDS

Words are wonderful. Just ask Lazarus. He was dead and buried. He was busy doing what believers do on the other side of the grave. Maybe he was fellowshipping with Samson, Daniel, Shadrach, and the other guys, when all of a sudden he heard those words. *"Lazarus, come forth!"* Lazarus had no choice but to come forth!

Some 2000 years ago, possibly the greatest three words ever uttered came from Jesus on the cross. He said, *"It is finished."* (John 19:30) We might wonder, just what was finished? God's plan for salvation was finished. No more sacrifice. No more unfulfilled demands of the law. No more anticipation of how the Messiah would take away sin. For Jesus…no more ministry. No more preaching. He had done what He was sent to do. The work of redemption was forever finished. God's plan of salvation was completed.

God alone initiates salvation and invites whosoever will to receive His only Son, Jesus Christ. Without Jesus, there is no plan of salvation. My salvation is not dependent upon my efforts to repent and turn from my sin. It is dependent upon how great God's grace is to cover my sin. His grace is greater than my sin. I know we believe that, but too often we are selective about whose sin God's grace will cover. We like the cleaned-up version of the prodigal, but I'm afraid he wouldn't be welcome in many churches in his far-country condition. When Jesus said it was finished, did He really mean that, or is there something we can do or must add to what He did? Friend, don't underestimate God's grace. He can save a man with a hateful heart as easily as He can a man with a lying tongue. Oswald Chambers said,

> "We trample the blood of the Son of God if we think we are forgiven because we are sorry for our sins. The only explanation for the forgiveness of God and for the unfathomable depth of His forgetting is the death of Jesus Christ.
>
> It does not matter who or what we are. There is absolute reinstatement into God by the death of Jesus Christ and by no other way, not because Jesus Christ pleads, but because He died. It is not earned but accepted."

It is finished. With His own blood, Jesus did what could never be done with the blood of bulls, goats, and rams. He accomplished what the law could never do. He finished and completed God's means of saving the lost. What He did was enough. There is no need for anything more to be done beyond what He did. It is forever finished.

"LAZARUS IS DEAD.": JOHN 11:14

The three words Mary and Martha never wanted to hear: *"Lazarus is dead."* He's not critically ill. He's not dying. His life is not in jeopardy. He has died. It is the unbelievable reality. The weeping begins. The questions without answers come. The Bible is full of death. It's a hard reality for loved ones to stand by, helplessly watching as a friend or family member slips off into eternity. Mary and Martha couldn't believe their ears. Lazarus was dead.

Several years ago I had the unfortunate responsibility as a pastor to minister to a family who had lost their mom and dad in a tragic automobile accident. These good people were more than just church members, they were some of my favorite people. The mother had died at the scene of the accident. Her husband was transported to the hospital where he died later that evening.

The waiting room was filled with family and friends from the church and community. Amazing things often happen in those places. Prayer becomes a priority, and no one cares who's listening or what they think or who might be offended that they're praying in Jesus' name. Believers began to embrace what they've always said they believed. That's when true Christians, regardless of their level of faith, began to stand on the promises of God and recall every scripture verse they've learned all the way back to when they were just children. Suddenly, people who disagree about politics and such put aside their differences and focus on things that really matter.

Late that evening, well after midnight, the doctor shared the news with the family that their dad had also died. Sure, there was weeping. But this weeping was different. For believers there is an unusual peace that, even in the midst of tears, God is good, Heaven is real, and salvation is sweet. Yes, believers weep, but not without hope. We know there is life beyond death and hope beyond the grave.

The deceiver, the Devil himself, would have us believe that the dead die never to live again. Some religious groups have bought into the false teaching that existence ends at the point of death, that there is no eternal life, that Jesus' resurrection is a hoax, and the story of Easter is a fairy tale. Think about what Dr. Al Mohler said:

> *"Without the resurrection of Jesus Christ from the dead, there is no Christianity and no salvation for sinners. If the resurrection is not true, then Christ is still in the grave and Christianity is false and deceptive. Worse, sinners have no hope of salvation and will face God's wrath. It is the very ground of the church's faith. Because He lives we can face tomorrow. Because He lives all fear is gone. Because He lives the disciples were willing to die. Because He lives the martyrs were willing to follow His example. If there is no resurrection, then close it up, sell the building, go home, eat, drink, and be merry for tomorrow we die.... If Christ merely died as a substitute for our sins, but remains in the grave, we remain in our sins. No resurrection, no salvation, no victory –- nothing! ...This is one of the non-negotiables of the faith; there is no way around the empty tomb. Skeptics throughout history have attempted to undermine Christianity by denying the resurrection because it is the lynchpin of the faith."*

His words stir me. He said, *"There is no way around the empty tomb."* Without the empty tomb we have no sermons to preach and no songs to sing. We have no hope here or in Heaven. There is no comfort, no consolation. Without the empty tomb we are doomed to despair. Without the resurrection our message falls apart. We can celebrate His birth, and be thankful for His death, but without the empty tomb we have no hope of eternal life. Mohler's words ought to make every believer unusually happy... unusually confident... because we are unusually blessed to have a

Savior such as Christ. I feel what the Samaritan woman must have felt when she went running through the streets telling everyone, *"Come see a man who's told me all I ever did."*

That night at the hospital while we were processing the news of the deaths of two people we loved dearly, if we ever believed in the resurrection, we believed that night. Don't get me wrong. There was no singing for joy, no happy faces, and no good news from the doctors. But something was good about this death. There was an unusual peace in the face of unbelievable tragedy. No one said anything about it. No announcement was made. But deep within all of us there was an unwavering confidence that just as Jesus was resurrected to new life, so will our friends be.

On another note, just recently I visited a dear lady who has been diagnosed with inoperable cancer. She's dying. On the front porch sitting with this frail yet faithful believer, I couldn't help but think about what lies ahead in the next few months. Without a miracle the doctors will soon say about her just what Jesus said about Lazarus. Death is coming. Without a miracle from God soon the doctors will be giving her a number of months or weeks until she passes. She said with utmost assurance, *"I'll be ok either way."* She sure will. She will either go to be with the Lord, or He will continue to be with her. She'll be all right. She believes in the resurrection.

Just because I believe in the resurrection doesn't mean I am required to enjoy the process of death and dying. As I write these words, I am once again reminded of my dad. He spent the last five years of his life confined to a nursing home facility. In his late eighties, with his memory fading and his body frail, I often wondered why God didn't take him home. My dad's best years were behind him, and his best life was ahead of him. Occasionally, on days when he was more talkative, I would ask him if he remembered the day he was saved. With a little help from me about the details, he recalled a Sunday morning when he gave his heart to the Lord. And he remembered the day I baptized him. These are good memories and wonderful reminders that the hope he had in Christ is a promise of life eternal. I enjoyed my dad as long as he lived here on earth, but I celebrated the day he left. I believe in the resurrection. I believe Jesus went to prepare a place for all who believe. I thank God my dad believed. And because he believed, he's in Heaven now.

One final thought about death. When a person dies the question is often asked, "Why did he die?" Especially when a person is young and in the prime of life, someone is bound to ask the question. Ultimately we can blame Adam. Look at 1 Cor. 15:22, *"For just as in Adam all die, so also in Christ all will be made alive."* The first Adam was made from the earth, but the Last Adam, which is Jesus, came from Heaven. Adam disobeyed God and brought sin and death into the world, but Jesus obeyed and brought righteousness and life to all who will believe.

Why did he die? We can blame the doctors. We can blame the sickness. Some folks will even blame God. Chances are when Lazarus died, there were some in the crowd who wanted to blame Jesus. But Jesus was not to blame for the death of Lazarus. He came to give life not take it. Death is a fact of life. Lazarus died, and eventually I'll die too. But I don't have to die without hope.

"DO YOU BELIEVE?": JOHN 11:26

"Do you believe?" This is the question that matters most. We ask many questions: "Why did Lazarus die?" "How did he die?" "When did he die?" "What if he hadn't died?" And there are many good points to ponder in the story of Lazarus. At the moment of death, however, the only thing that matters is: "Do you believe?" At that moment, whether or not a person believed in Christ and trusted Him with their life is all that matters. Not why, when, or how. But did they believe?

Go with me for a minute to the graveside of a loved one. Stand with me beneath the tent, surrounded by flowers, comforted by family and friends, with a preacher reading from the Bible. What do you believe?

I have stood at gravesides with grieving families in the heat of July as well as the cold of January. I have read the story of Lazarus on most of those occasions. At times the temperature was so hot it was almost unbearable. At other times the temperature hovered around freezing. I've stood under a tent while it was raining, and I've stood in wind that was so strong I had to brace myself. But the heat and the cold and the rain and wind have no effect on what we believe. Whether I am reading the story of Lazarus while shivering from the cold or while wiping sweat, my beliefs are certain. The grave is not the end. Jesus arose and so will everyone who believes in Him for salvation. And the question I always ask the grieving family… *"Do you believe?"* Because what you believe about death and eternity changes everything.

I believe this is the question we all must answer. Do you really believe what you've always said you believe? All the retreats, Bible conferences, summer camps, revival meetings, Sunday School classes, and Bible studies can't help you if at that moment when death comes you don't believe. Scripture memorization, knowing what the Bible says, understanding the original languages of the Bible, and even understanding the historical and theological context of the scriptures is absolutely wonderful. But if you can't believe in the resurrection hope found only in Christ, what hope do you have? If the grave is the end, there is no hope beyond death. I believe we should sing of the resurrection and preach the resurrection. But may God help us above all to believe in and hold dear the resurrection of the dead. Our hope is built on nothing less than Christ and His resurrection.

You can say you believe the Bible. You may say you believe what Baptists believe, or what Methodists believe, or that you're conservative or liberal, or whatever label you place on yourself. You may say you believe in Jesus. But do you believe what He said? What do you believe about Him? The Mormons, Jehovah's Witnesses, and Muslims believe in Jesus. In James 2:19 we read, *"Even the demons believe and tremble."* Why did James include that in his writing? Why is it important to know that demons believe? I think James is making a point by using sarcasm. In an attempt to make light of these believers' weak show of faith, he sheds light on the faith of demons. Even the demons believe in the resurrection. The demons were there on the morning of the third day. They saw it all. That's why they tremble.

Think about that, *"Even the demons believe..."* Demons believe in Jesus. Does the Devil himself believe in Jesus? Yes! In fact I think the Devil believes in Jesus more than many Christians do. Why is that? Satan was there at the cross and also on the morning of the resurrection. He knows more than anyone that Jesus was dead and buried but came back to life. Demons tremble because they know death couldn't hold Him. He withstood their greatest assault. He overcame the grave. He's coming again to rescue the church. He is the resurrection and the life. His name is above every name. That'll make a demon tremble.

I've been preaching and pastoring for most of my life. I've heard just about every weird belief you can imagine. I've talked to saints and sinners alike. I've listened as they told me what they believed and what they didn't believe. I have discovered there are four distinct groups of believers out there in our churches. See if you recognize any of these folks.

BELIEVERS WHO DON'T BELIEVE...

These are the folks in our churches and communities who have a Bible and respect it as an important book. But they don't believe what it says. They acknowledge the need for church, yet they seldom attend. They believe there is a God, yet that belief has no impact on their daily living. They believe prayer is important, yet they never pray. Ask them if they believe in these things, they'll say, "yes." But their lifestyle says, "no." Repentance, faith, and trust in Christ all lead to a change of heart and life. The Bible calls it a transformation. It's more than being religious; it's becoming a new creation. It's one thing to <u>believe in God</u>, it's another thing to <u>believe God</u> and be changed.

I hesitate to refer to these unbelieving believers as *believers*. It's almost like they're unsaved Christians. They have values and strong views on things like politics, traditions, and the moral decline of society. But what they believe regarding the things of God has no impact on their life. They might say that going to church is good but not necessary for a person to go to Heaven. They might think prayer is good at times for those who need such a thing. They often come across as a little bit Christian, a little agnostic, and little atheistic. They might think it's a good thing for their children to be christened, confirmed, or baptized. But to take up their cross daily, deny themselves, and follow Christ sounds a little fanatical. Theirs is a surface Christianity that is Christian in name only. They believe in God just enough to say they believe. But what they believe about God has little if any effect on how they live. Know anyone like that?

BELIEVERS WHO DON'T KNOW WHAT TO BELIEVE...

These are folks who have been overwhelmed by church options and religious information. They're always asking questions, always seeking answers, reading every new book, following every new movement, yet they're not sure what they think about Jesus. Our world is full of them. They have believed what Grandmother believed. They have agreed with their uncle's preacher. They have been saved and saved again and again. The own a copy of the Book of Mormon. They have a copy of the Koran. And they have a few copies of the Bible. They can quote a few verses of scripture. They still have the Bible they received when they were baptized, but they've never read it. They started out strong but may have gotten overwhelmed with options and differing denominational viewpoints and soon they were underwhelmed and gave up. They don't know what to believe so they end up believing not much of anything.

I had a conversation with a man recently that had gotten saved in his late thirties after running from God for a number of years. His wife convinced him to go to church with her. He went, heard the Gospel, and was saved. He gave up his drinking and profanity. With tears in his eyes he told me he knew he was saved. He said God changed his heart and his life. He was a new believer. He had very little Bible knowledge. He didn't realize the different beliefs among Christians. At that time, if someone had asked him to find a passage of scripture in the book of Acts he would have had to look in the table of contents.

One day, with his new-found faith and joy in his heart, he walked into a store in his small hometown to do some shopping. He noticed a Bible verse on a sign in the window. He walked in and said, *"So you folks are Christians?...So am I!"* They asked what church he attended and what his salvation experience was like. After he shared with them his story, they responded by telling him he wasn't really saved. They quoted scripture to support their beliefs, but it was confusing to this thirty-nine-year-old new believer. It was a little overwhelming. The church he attended had noticed his zeal for the Lord and suggested he teach a Bible study class. But he was still a young believer. He still had a very limited understanding of the scriptures. He accepted the challenge, however, and began teaching a Bible study. He was overwhelmed again by all the questions he couldn't answer, as well as all the disagreements among those in the class. To make a long story short, he eventually gave up teaching and gradually got out of church and away from God. When I spoke to him he was in his early sixties, out of church, and not sure what he believed.

The man in that story is, I believe, one of thousands. Overwhelmed and then underwhelmed. Confused and disappointed. Hopeful and then hopeless. Oh friend, may God help us to be careful how we treat and what we say to new believers. May God help us to be careful about putting someone in a leadership position that hasn't matured in their walk with God. Because people like the man I just described are everywhere, and they honestly don't know what to believe.

BELIEVERS WHO WILL BELIEVE ANYTHING...

These are folks who are as comfortable in a Mormon temple as they are in a Baptist church. They're not offended by your beliefs. They agree with you. They agree with everyone. Their favorite saying is: "Why can't we all just get along?" They've been sprinkled and immersed. They're both liberal and fundamental. I lived near a lady like this several years ago. When I met her she was a member of a Baptist church. She had been raised Roman Catholic. She had also been a Jehovah's Witness. Not long after I met her, she had joined the local Assembly of God. She believed it all. That reminds me of a funeral service I was asked to participate in when I was a student in New Orleans. The service was in an Assembly of God building. Both preachers were Baptist. The lady who had passed away held rosary beads in her hands. Friends, we are surrounded by good people who'll believe anything.

These believers who will believe anything reminds me of Solomon Stoddard and the Half-Way Covenant in New England in the early 1730's. At that time a person was only allowed to receive the Lord's Supper if they had been converted to Christ. Stoddard urged other pastors to allow morally upright people to receive communion even though they were unsaved in hopes that they would be saved. Initially the Half-Way Covenant appeared to work in bringing many people to Christ. But over time the unconverted church members began to have great influence. Their influence caused the church to suffer because of the neglect of spiritual matters. Solomon Stoddard's grandson was Jonathan Edwards. He saw the problems the Half-Way Covenant was creating in the church. Because of the great number and undeniable influence of the unsaved church members, Edwards knew something had to be done to stop the wave of compromise. Over time, as Edwards was led by the Holy Spirit in his preaching, revival came and many of those unsaved church members were saved (Elmer Towns: The Ten Greatest Revivals Ever).

Believers in Christ can't believe just anything and remain right with God. It is a narrow way that leads to Christ. Believers can't believe in Christ and Mohammad. Jesus said He was the way, the truth, and the life, and that no man could come to the Father but by Him. (John 14:6) In Acts 4:12 Peter boldly preached, *"…there is no other name under Heaven given among men by which we must be saved."* In Colossians 1:27 Paul writes of, *"…Christ in you, the hope of glory."* Our hope is in Christ alone. And because of that, it matters that we place our trust in Him alone.

BELIEVERS WHO BELIEVE...

These are folks who believe God and His word. They may not always understand the Bible, but they believe it. These folks may not always understand God, but they trust Him. Their life has been radically changed through a personal relationship with Christ. They have been saved by the grace of God. They are led by the Holy Spirit. Most of these folks have never been to seminary and never understood Greek or Hebrew. But they believe. They believe by faith. They are kind, compassionate, and Christ-like. Friend, if you don't believe by faith, you will never believe. Without faith, God is unbelievable.

I believe in the Grand Canyon, but I've never been there. I've seen pictures and heard what others say about it. To know Christ we must do more than believe what others say. We must do more than enjoy the pictures. We have to go there. I would love to go and experience the Grand Canyon, but that may never happen. However, I can go to God and experience Him anytime or all the time. Believers who really believe are those who have come to Jesus and have trusted Him to take away their sin. They've recognized their inability to save themselves. In some way they have called on His name. They've confessed their sin, turned from their sin, and believed in His name alone for forgiveness. They're far from perfect, but they are redeemed. They have confessed Christ with their mouth and have believed in their heart that God has raised Jesus from the dead. They believe in what God did and what He will do. These are believers who believe.

THINK ABOUT THESE VERSES...

John 11:15 "*And I am glad for your sakes that I was not there, that you may believe. Nevertheless let us go to him.*" This is a troubling verse. In these days of believing things like, "God will never disappoint you..." and "God will always be there for you..." this verse deals a painful blow to that kind of thinking. Don't miss this. Jesus was glad He was not there when Lazarus died. That's a little uncomfortable. His hope was that their faith would survive, even thrive, that they might *believe* during these few days of His absence. His hope was that Mary and Martha's faith would be increased and that unbelievers would become believers because of the miracle of Lazarus' resurrection.

Here's a hard pill to swallow: If you really believe, you'll believe even if Jesus doesn't come when you call Him. Again, even when the prayer isn't answered the way you had hoped, when your prodigal doesn't come home, when the cancer comes back, when the unimaginable becomes reality, you'll still believe. I sure wish I could put a more positive spin on Jesus' absence. I wish I had a more positive answer for the reason He was not there.

Having flown in and out of Atlanta many times over the years, once or twice I have been on a plane that was put in a holding pattern. We simply flew around until our landing was cleared. I could see the airport where we would land. We just couldn't land yet. We were waiting in a holding pattern. Think about that phrase, *"holding pattern."* Sometimes, I am convinced God puts us in a holding pattern. And it is a pattern, a design, a clear map designed by the Lord. But there are days when His pattern feels like a prison. Mary and Martha must have felt much the same. They knew where Jesus was. They knew if He were there Lazarus would not die. They could see the airport, they just couldn't land. Friend, if you find yourself in a similar situation, a crisis, a difficult circumstance, and Jesus doesn't show up like you thought He would, don't give up on Him. He'll be there when you need him.

John 11:27 *"She said to Him, 'Yes, Lord, I believe that you are the Christ, the Son of God, who is to come into the world.'"* Most of us won't believe in God like we should until we survive some life-changing event. Maybe you'll survive a heart attack or a stroke. Maybe you'll survive a battle with cancer. Maybe you'll survive a tragic automobile accident. Maybe you'll win your battle with alcohol. Maybe someone you love will survive a close encounter with death. After the storm is passed, you'll believe like you've never believed before.

In this passage Jesus was speaking to Martha. She didn't need a life-changing event to help her believe. But you can be sure the death and resurrection of Lazarus caused her to believe in a way she had never believed. I saw a lady not long ago that had on a shirt with the words, *"I'm A Survivor."* I thought to myself, "I need one of those." Maybe you do, too. Most folks have survived something. The church is filled with survivors. Survivors have scars. They have war stories. There's a miracle in every pew and there's a story behind every scar. Mary and Martha and Lazarus would have a story to tell. Because they believed when it was hard to believe. A few verses later when Mary received word that Jesus was coming, she ran out of the house where a crowd was gathered. They thought she was running to the grave to weep there. I love this part of the story. Instead of running to the grave, she ran to Jesus. Friend, if you're discouraged about what you're facing, and you feel like all hope is gone, don't give up. Don't run to the grave and weep. Run to Jesus.

John 11:40 *"Jesus said to her, 'Did I not say to you that if you would believe you would see the glory of God?'"* Don't you just love the way Jesus took control of the situation? Yes, He could have prevented all this by healing Lazarus before he even died. But He had a greater plan in mind. He had been absent so that they *"Would see the glory of God."* In this passage Jesus has just commanded that the stone be rolled away. Martha had stated the obvious. I can hear her now, "Lord, if you'd been here He wouldn't be dead. Just leave him alone. It's too late."

How about you? Have you ever given God advice? I have. As if I knew better. As if I could instruct Him. As if my will was greater than His. Yes, I have prayed too many prayers that were more like instructions than petitions. As I look back at all those selfish prayers I prayed when I was worried, fearful, doubtful, hurt, angry, I am so glad God didn't answer the way I prayed He would. If the Lord had listened to Martha, Lazarus would have remained in the grave and Martha would have missed seeing the glory of God. I wonder how often we miss God's glory because of our unbelief. Because of our impatience. Because of our frustration. Because of our anger with God. Martha saw the glory of God. And so will we - if we will believe.

John 11:42-43 *"And I know that you always hear me, but because of the people who are standing by I said this, that they may believe that You sent Me."* In this passage Jesus is thanking His heavenly Father. He is thanking God for hearing Him, *"that they may believe."* Jesus came to save sinners. I think His plan was that this miracle resurrection would cause others to believe that God had sent Him. That they might believe that He alone was the Messiah, the one who could take away sin.

He thanked God for what would happen before it even happened. He thanked God while Lazarus was still dead. Don't miss this simple, yet obvious truth: Jesus believed in God. He believed in His Heavenly Father. There was a lot on the line here. What if Jesus called out for Lazarus to come forth and nothing happened? Needless to say that would have given those who didn't believe more reason not to believe. Here's a great place to ask the question, "What would Jesus do?" He would believe. He did believe. God, help us to believe like Jesus.

John 11:48 *"If we let Him alone like this, everyone will believe in Him, and the Romans will come and take away both our place and nation."* The chief priests and Pharisees began to concoct a plan to put Jesus to death. Chief priests and Pharisees never got along with Jesus. They always found fault and quoted some aspect of the law that not even they were keeping. And He always exposed their hypocrisy. Don't be surprised, even in our day, when religious leaders seek to do away with Jesus, silence Christians, and close churches. Billy Graham once said, *"If Jesus were to come today just as He did two thousand years ago, He would be crucified in less time than He was then."*

As I write these words, our nation is in the midst of "cancel culture," an effort to erase history and rewrite the narrative of America's history. Part of this effort to cancel culture involves tearing down monuments and statues dedicated to the memory of good men and women who gave their lives for American freedom. There is also an effort to cancel Christianity. Some are even tearing down statues of Christ. It's a sad day we are living in. But here's the good news: though the monuments of Christianity are torn down, the message of Christ will never be destroyed. The chief priests thought they could get rid of Jesus by killing Him, but they never imagined the resurrection. Men and women have died, churches have been burned, and monuments have been destroyed. But from my point of view, all these attempts to destroy the message only make it stronger. You simply can't cancel Christ.

"LAZARUS COME FORTH!": JOHN 11:43

Why not leave Lazarus in the grave? He's at peace. He's no longer sick. He's in a better place. He would eventually grow older and die again. Martha and Mary would weep again. There would be another funeral and another burial. From a common sense point of view one must ask, why bring him back? There seem to be two wonderful reasons, both of which defy common sense.

THIS IS FOR THE GLORY OF GOD...

One thing is clear in John 11:4: this was not done for the glory of Lazarus. It was done for the glory of God. This was not about Lazarus. This was about the power of God. If this had been about Lazarus, we would probably have a book in the Bible that bears his name. If this had been about Lazarus, Jesus would have told us so. For instance, when Jesus described John the Baptist, He wasn't short on superlatives. He said John the Baptist was the greatest man ever born of woman. That's pretty great, wouldn't you say? So when Jesus says nothing about Lazarus' greatness in this story, His silence speaks volumes. This resurrection wasn't about the greatness of Lazarus. It was about the greatness of God.

Have you ever stopped to think about all we go through as believers and why God allows us to go through such difficulties and hardships? Lazarus' story wasn't about Lazarus, and our story isn't about us. We are tempted to make it about us, but our story is for His glory. As much as we try to write our story, God is holding the pen. God wrote the story of Lazarus for His own glory. The story of our lives is being written for the sole purpose of bringing glory to God. Think about it. How has God used your struggles to draw people to Himself? Trouble and heartache are facts of life. But God uses those things to show us His love and to reveal His power. The whole story of the death, burial, and resurrection of Lazarus was for the glory of God.

That the Son of God might be glorified...

To all the skeptics and critics of Jesus, this one reason was of premium importance. Many of those who didn't believe in Jesus had no problem believing in a heavenly Father. So this reasoning was a slap in the face of those Pharisees who thought themselves equal to Christ. This miracle of Lazarus was not only accomplished for the glory of God, but in particular that Jesus might be glorified. That JESUS would be glorified.

After Jesus had raised him there was no doubt about his power. Lazarus must be sick and die, that Christ may be glorified as the Lord of life. The resurrection is the foundation of what we are and all we believe as Christians. We sing about it. It's the basis of all we teach and preach. It's the message of missionaries in foreign countries. We believe in the unbelievable, Jesus raises the dead. Our hope is built on Him. Our hope is in Him. Our hope is because of Him alone.

As I try to bring this chapter to a close, there is so much more I want to say. There were other hopeless cases in scripture that were just as critical as that of Lazarus.

Taking into consideration that Lazarus was already dead and buried, think about these other hopeless situations and how God did the unthinkable. The question Jesus asked that day just before the resurrection of Lazarus still rings loudly, *"Do you believe?"*

The Gadarene demoniac was already bound with chains.

Look at Mark 5:1-13. There is no bondage so great that God cannot break it. The demoniac could not be tamed. Maybe that's you, or your son or daughter, or your husband or wife. There is a power greater than demons. Greater than addictions and struggles. Listen friend, we either believe God can break our chains of bondage or not. Most of us who believe have experienced His power in some undeniable way. Most of us have been faced with a problem that was bigger and stronger than we could manage on our own. So big and strong that only God could break its power. Friend, if you are being held captive by something that is greater than your power to resist, why don't you trust God with it? Why not turn it over to Him? Believe that He's greater than your problem. Don't believe it? The Gadarene demoniac probably didn't either.

Jairus' daughter was already dead.

Look at Mark 5:21-24, 35-42. Notice the things Jesus did. In verse 24, "...*So Jesus went with him.*" This was not a detour. This was part of Jesus' plan for the day. In verse 37, "*He permitted only Peter James and John...*" In verse 40 "*...When He had put them all aside...*" Jesus took control of the situation. He went to where she was, taking with him some men of faith. And when He had put out all the doubters and unbelievers, He walked in and she walked out.

Imagine Jesus going in and then coming back out saying, "Folks, I'm sorry but there's nothing I can do..." We can rest assured of this: Jesus has never faced a situation He couldn't reverse. He has never met a sickness He couldn't heal. When Jesus walks in the room, everything changes.

Don't you just love stories like this? Because most of us have read the Bible a few times and already have an understanding of Jesus and His healing power, this story may not stir us like it would someone who reads it for the first time. You can imagine the suspense that day, especially when Jesus asked the unbelievers to step outside. This story still packs a punch for those who are reading it for the first time. What will Jesus do? How will this end? Nothing has changed. We may not be like Jairus and his daughter, but we all face situations only God can reverse. We may not know what He will do or how He will do it. But by faith, we believe He will always do what's best.

Bartimaeus was already blind.

Look at Mark 10:46-52. Notice in verse 51 Jesus asked, *"What do you want me to do for you?"* That's a good question. That's a wonderful question. In fact, that's the greatest question that Jesus could have asked. Bartimaeus was faced with the opportunity of a lifetime. What did he want Jesus to do for him? What did he want more than anything? This was his moment. This was the turning point in the life of a man who had no hope of ever seeing again.

What do you want the Lord to do for you? What could Jesus do for you that would make your life complete? I certainly don't want to be too simplistic, but maybe you should tell the Lord about what you want Him to do for you. And while you're at it, ask Him what He wants you to do for Him. Like an old Gospel song says, *"Are you weary? Are you heavy hearted? Tell it to Jesus."* Tell Him what you want more than anything and then be willing to do what He says. Don't live your life with regrets. By the way, Bartimaeus must have meant business. He was serious. He *"cast aside his garment. He arose and came to Jesus."* Why don't you?

This chapter has been about words…three words. Let's take a minute to backtrack. We thought about the words, *"Lazarus is dead."* Then we looked at the words, *"Do you believe?"* Finally we celebrated the greatest words Lazarus ever heard, *"Lazarus, come forth."* It's absolutely amazing how three simple words can change everything.

But there was another resurrection that changed the world forever. And before we leave this thought, I want to remind you of some of the greatest words ever spoken. Read Matthew 28:5-7 and enjoy....

Don't Be Afraid.

He's Not Here.

He Is Risen.

3

TWO SISTERS

They didn't run to the tomb. They ran to Jesus.

John 11:21,32

They say no two people are alike. I'll say "amen" to that. You'll hear comparisons between brothers and sisters, "They're like daylight and dark," "She's nothing like her sister," and "He's nothing like his brother." People are different. Like the two sisters, Mary and Martha.

In the story of Lazarus, Mary and Martha were ordinary sisters who possessed extraordinary faith. Their confidence and tenacity is what we hope to have when we face the death of a loved one. When their world was falling apart, they didn't. They demonstrated a gritty courage – in different ways, but neither seemed to waiver during these four days of curve balls and bombshells. Lazarus is sick unto death. Lazarus died. Jesus appears to be late. When their faith in God could have died, it increased. When they could have given up, they looked up.

This is an interesting story because it appears Jesus was good friends with Martha, Mary, and Lazarus. I wish we knew more about Jesus' relationship with these two sisters and their brother. I wish we knew more about how they became friends. We simply don't know more than what the scriptures tell us. But I think we can safely use our imaginations.

As I mentioned earlier, a number of years ago I was a student at New Orleans Baptist Theological Seminary. Those were wonderful days for me. I was young and had my life ahead of me. God used those days to begin shaping and molding me for the life and ministry before me. I was impressed to move onto the campus in New Orleans after hearing Dr. Don Wilton preach. He was one of the professors in New Orleans at that time. I became friends with Dr. Wilton and, after much prayer, I was soon living on the seminary campus. I had always heard that I'd make friends for life while at seminary. I looked forward to that, but those first few weeks on campus I didn't have anyone other than Dr. Wilton that I considered a friend. That all changed one day while I was having a cup of coffee between classes.

Roc Collins walked into the cafeteria. I remember seeing a bright orange blur come through the door. Roc was wearing the brightest and shiniest Tennessee jacket I have ever seen in my life. The orange jacket, with Roc in it, made its way over to the table where I was seated. I was having coffee with Dr. Wilton, and he called for Roc to come over. He introduced us to each other and then said to Roc about me, *"He's one of us."* I didn't really know what that meant at the time, but I sure liked it. I know what it means now. It didn't mean we all shared a love for Tennessee football. It didn't mean we were all members of the bright orange jacket club. It meant we shared a passion for preaching. I was one of *them.*

It's been almost thirty years since I graduated from New Orleans Seminary, but I am glad to say I am still one of them. I'm still friends with Dr. Wilton and Roc, and I still have a passion to preach. When Jesus first met Martha, Mary, and Lazarus, I like to imagine He said to His disciples, "They're one of us." Grammatically that doesn't sound right, but you get the idea. There was an immediate bond. There was an instant connection. My friend Roc and I have shared that for years. And I believe Jesus, Martha, Mary, and Lazarus shared a common bond. They were seeking and believing God. And when the three siblings found Christ, they followed Him.

Can you imagine what that relationship might have been like? Can you imagine walking and talking with Jesus every day? Can you imagine asking Him anything you wanted to know? Can you imagine being in His presence each day? Imagine Him being your best friend. Friend, that kind of relationship doesn't take an imagination. It takes faith and trust and obedience. We can walk and talk with Him every day.

Here's a page from the past for many of us who were raised on the old hymns of the church.

> *"What a friend we have in Jesus, all our sins and griefs to bear!*
> *What a privilege to carry everything to God in prayer!*
> *O what peace we often forfeit, O what needless pain we bear.*
> *All because we do not carry, everything to God in prayer.*
>
> *Have we trials and temptations? Is there trouble anywhere?*
> *We should never be discouraged, take it to the Lord in prayer.*
> *Can we find a friend so faithful, who will all our sorrows share?*
> *Jesus knows our every weakness; take it to the Lord in prayer.*
>
> *Are we weak and heavy laden, cumbered with a load of care?*
> *Precious Savior, still our refuge, take it to the Lord in prayer.*

Do thy friends despise, forsake thee? Take it to the Lord in prayer!
In His arms He'll take and shield thee; thou wilt find a solace there.

That wonderful old hymn has an amazing history. According to *101 Hymn Stories* by Kenneth Osbeck and *Then Sings My Soul* by Robert Morgan, the hymn was originally nothing more than a poem scribbled on paper. When Joseph Scriven learned of his mother's serious illness and realizing he would not be able to be with her because of the great distance, he wrote a letter to her that included the words that eventually became the hymn, "What A Friend We Have In Jesus."

Sometime later when he became sick, a visiting friend noticed the words he had written on a small piece of paper by his bedside. His friend asked if he had written the words. Scriven replied, *"The Lord and I did it between us."*

Chances are that one of the greatest hymns ever written came from a simple poem scribbled on scrap paper. But it was more than his mother's sickness that inspired this great hymn. At age twenty-five, Scriven decided to leave his family and move to Canada. His reasons for leaving seem to have been his religious beliefs. These beliefs separated him from those who loved him most and those on whom he could lean in troubled times. Even though he was true to his convictions, he undoubtedly missed his family.

Also influential in his writing the words to the hymn was the death of his fiancée the night before their scheduled wedding. Scriven eventually fell in love with another woman. But heartache came again for him when his bride to be died of tuberculosis before their wedding could take place (Source: Cargill, Osbeck, Morgan).

Needless to say, Joseph Scriven knew something about having a friend in Jesus. And following the events of Lazarus' death, burial, and resurrection, Mary and Martha knew Jesus in a way that most of us never will. He was more than a healer. He was more than One with power over death. More than One who works miracles. They knew Him as an amazing friend. A friend like no other. He is such a friend. Many of you who read these words know the Lord as someone who sticks closer than a brother. Someone who is a friend of sinners. O, what a friend He is!

I have a friend named Ralph that I admire greatly. Ralph is old enough to be my dad but I've never really given the age difference much thought. My admiration for him grew out of watching Ralph respond to the death of his son and his wife just months apart. The death of his son was sudden and unexpected. The passing of his wife came after an extended illness. I was Ralph's pastor for a number of years. I watched as he pressed on after the loss of his son and wife. I watched as he leaned on the Lord, as he believed and rested in his hope in Jesus. Several years have passed now since their passing but Ralph's faith hasn't wavered. I believe it is because my friend had found a friend in Jesus.

MARTHA

Martha was a worker, busy doing what needed to be done. You've seen people like her. They're better if they're busy. They can't sit still. They sleep little, if any. They rise early and stay up late. The more they do, the more content they are. However, the truth for some folks is that being busy is an admirable but not necessarily good quality. Some folks can be so busy in the Lord's work that that they miss the work of the Lord. They can get so busy doing that they ignore being. Like some of us preachers, we get so wrapped up in the sermon that we miss the message. The point being, it's not as important how much I do for the Lord as it is how much I love the One I'm doing it for. The priority is not how much I serve Him as it is how much I love Him. It's not what I do. It's why I do what I do.

Martha was the first to meet Jesus after the death of Lazarus. She does two things upon meeting Him. She questions His absence and affirms her faith (John 11:20-22). We'll look at that in greater detail later, but for now let's think about the qualities that set Martha apart from Mary.

MARTHA WORKED: LUKE 10:40

The scriptures tell us Martha was distracted by her many tasks. Many writers have described her busy-ness in the form of criticism. We could find many reasons to criticize people like her. They're so busy they often neglect others and even themselves so they can complete the task at hand. But before we get too critical, let's be honest—the church needs Martha. She'll make sure everything's ready. She'll come early to be sure preparations have been made, and she'll stay late to be sure all is cleaned up. She'll attempt anything. If you need a volunteer, she's the first one to raise her hand. She'll cook, clean, teach, and paint. Do you know anyone like her?

Martha was a hard worker, but look at what she missed. She missed the opportunity to simply sit at Jesus' feet. Maybe I am a little like her in this regard. Sitting at Jesus' feet is not for everyone. I'm not saying we don't need to be still and meditate sitting at His feet. It's just that some of us feel closer to God when we are serving rather than sitting. Take a minute to understand what I'm about to say. Some of the godliest women I've ever known were more at home in the church nursery changing diapers than they were in a classroom leading a Bible study. Some of those ladies were more comfortable standing at a kitchen stove, or painting a preschool classroom, or driving a senior adult to their doctor's appointment than they were "sitting at Jesus' feet." The whole idea of "sitting" doesn't fit Martha and other women like her. Don't be too critical of Martha. If she has the choice of sitting or serving, she'll be the one serving.

But I also have to admit there is something to be said of sitting. We're often too busy to sit. Yes, it has much to do with our personality type, but many of us would rather take matters into our own hands than trust someone else with the outcome. We fret too much. We would do well to take a deep breath. We need to sit down and listen to God. As much as I like to be busy, I probably need to be more like Mary. I need to sit down, rest in Him, and listen to Him.

MARTHA WORRIED: LUKE 10:41

Jesus himself told her she was worried about too many things. Some translations describe "worried" as "bothered," "concerned about," or "troubled." Martha had a lot on her mind. Jesus said an important thing to her. He said there was really only one thing that mattered. Mary had found it...Martha missed it. What was it that Martha missed? I am not sure, but I believe the good thing Martha missed and Mary found was uninterrupted time with Jesus. I think that's it. Unhindered time with Him. The truth with many of us is that we miss the simple quietness of time spent with Jesus. Especially folks like Martha. She was making a fuss about too many things.

While I want to commend those who work and serve faithfully, we can't overlook the obvious. It's one thing to be a worker. It's another to be a worrier. To be a person who allows worry, even perfectionism, to control their life. If that describes any of us, may God help us to stop making a fuss about things that do not matter. Find a quiet place and sit at Jesus' feet. We may not have as much time to do that as we think.

Chuck Swindoll says worrying is, *"assuming responsibility for things that are out of our control"* (insight.org), Worry is a thief stealing our peace of mind. Worry is a murderer killing our joy. Worry is a slave master binding heavy loads on us that we cannot bear. Worry is a heckler shouting doubt and fear. Worry is a mocker making light of our faith in God. Oh, if we could only heed 1 Peter 5:7, *"Cast all your cares on Him because He cares for you…"* Friend, once again may I suggest finding a quiet spot and do some casting…cast your cares on Jesus. The songwriter said it best, *"Oh yes, He cares. I know He cares. His heart is touched with my grief."* (Frank Graeff)

MARTHA WATCHED: JOHN 11:21

I remember as a four or five-year-old boy watching for my father to get home from work. In the summer months I would sit on the front porch and wait until I could hear him coming, and then I would run to meet him at the end of the driveway. My father drove a pickup truck with mud tires on the back. There was a distinct roar when he got within a mile or so of our home. I knew it was him. Why was I so excited to see him and run to the end of our driveway to meet him? Because he would let me drive. That's right. He'd sit me in his lap and the steering wheel was all mine. Daddy let me drive. That's why I was watching for him.

Martha was watching for Jesus. I imagine Martha was impatient, fidgeting, scurrying around, and almost exasperated over the idea that Jesus was not where she thought He should be. In our day, she would have been texting and phoning trying to find the location of Jesus. She would have already sent out a Facebook alert asking all her friends to be on the lookout. That was then. This is now. Then, all she had was hope. And hope in Christ is really all we have now. When you strip a person of wealth, health, and material possessions – when a person is down to their last dime and their last friend, if they have faith in Jesus, there is still hope. Martha had hope that Jesus would soon return. Hope that He could change everything. Hope that Jesus really was who she believed He was. So she waited and watched and hoped.

There's something to be said about watching for Jesus. But maybe Martha, and we too, can learn something from Mary once again. Mary remained seated in the house. While I write these words I am saying to myself, "If I am in this story, I'm with Martha." That's right. I'd like to think that I'd be like Mary, cool, calm, and collected. But if I know me, I'm running with Martha to see Jesus. It's like hearing the mud tires on my dad's truck. It's like me as a five-year-old boy seeing the blinker on Dad's truck, knowing he'd soon be turning in and I'd soon be behind the wheel. As a young boy I couldn't wait! Oh, if we could only harness our anxiety and run to Jesus, confidently throwing ourselves at His feet. I believe the church is a better place with both Mary and Martha being who they are. We need folks who are calm under pressure. And we need Martha who'll watch anxiously for the return of Jesus.

MARY

Mary is found three times in the Gospels, and each time she is at Jesus' feet. In Luke 10:39 she sat at His feet and listened to Him speak. Like a sponge Mary soaked up the words of Christ. In John 11:32 she fell at His feet and poured out her sorrow. In complete desperation and in utter despair, she fell on her knees. Don't miss the message here. Jesus was her only hope. She fell at *His* feet. This alone is evidence of her faith. She fell at His feet and no one else's. He was all she had, her only source of hope. In John 12:3 she knelt at His feet to give Him her praise and worship. She anointed His feet and wiped them with her hair. The old Gospel song rings true in this passage, "Little Is Much

When God Is In It." Mary had little to offer, but she did what she could with what she had.

MARY WORSHIPPED: LUKE 10:39

Jesus told Martha that Mary was doing a good thing, sitting at His feet listening to what He had to say. Just a few paragraphs ago you read that some people are more comfortable serving than sitting. But Jesus said Mary was doing a good thing. What's so great about sitting at Jesus' feet?

Some of you have spent many days and nights at the feet of Jesus. You didn't plan on it, but tragic and heartbreaking circumstances led you to a place of desperation. It was more quality God-time than you ever dreamed you'd have. You were placed in a situation you didn't see coming. Maybe you had a child so sick that even the doctors were discouraged. Or maybe you had a teen so troubled that you questioned your sanity, as well as your ability to be a parent. Or maybe you spent most of your life with an abusive husband or with an adulterous wife, and you know the heartache of not having your dreams come true. Or maybe you were sick or depressed or physically limited all your life, and you have learned to lean on Jesus out of necessity.

2020 was a year that will undoubtedly produce some great writings and recordings. It was a year of chaos and calamity. A year of weeping and wondering what the future would hold. Due to the impact of the pandemic Covid 19, we all lost friends and loved ones. We all found ourselves quarantined for a week or two. We grew anxious as businesses and churches closed their doors. We didn't know who to trust. We didn't know what to believe. It drew many into the presence of God. It called many of us to the feet of Jesus. To pray. Plead. Grieve. Seek. While the altars were empty in most churches, I am convinced there were crowds at His feet. And yes, in the days to come I believe we will hear many great hymns, choruses, and praises that were written during such a time of crisis. And we will no doubt read the works of poets, playwrights, and authors who put pen to paper expressing the heart cries of a nation.

Worship doesn't necessarily involve choirs and preaching. Worship can be you and God alone in a quiet place. It may involve no songs and no sermon. Just you and the Lord. Or maybe just you and the piano. Just you and a guitar. Just you in a quiet place beneath the shade of an old tree. Like a fella told me once, *"Preacher, sometimes I have more church in my truck with just me and the Lord than I do in church on a pew."* Worship can happen anywhere and anytime you call on God. Like the Lord said to Mary, that is a *"good thing."* That's what Mary chose to do. If Mary was feeling a little sassy she might suggest to Martha, put up your broom, and get out your Bible. Or maybe, God is more concerned about your heart than He is about your house. Or maybe, there'll be time enough to prepare the food. While we can, let's sit at His feet. Charles Wesley said it like this:

> *"Faithful to my Lord's commands,*
> *I still would choose the better part;*
> *Serve with careful Martha's hands,*
> *And loving Mary's heart."*

Think about that - Martha's hands and Mary's heart. And before we criticize either of them, let's realize how God needs each of them and each of us whether we're more comfortable setting the table or sitting at His feet. God has a place and a purpose for each of us.

MARY WAITED: JOHN 11:28-31

Unlike Martha, who was fretting, Mary sat quietly and waited on the Lord. Most of us have waited and worried and wondered how much longer we'd have to wait. We've waited on children, parents, doctors, for stores to open, and for parks to close. As I've said before, we've waited in waiting rooms, on interstates, and under umbrellas. We may not have enjoyed most of the waiting we've done, but Jesus seemed to think that Mary's waiting was a good thing.

In 1 Samuel 30:6, David had led his men astray. Away from God and into a war they had no business fighting, they returned from battle to find their village in Ziklag had been destroyed by the Amalekites. Their women and children had also been carried away captive. David's army was angry, to say the least. Not only were they upset with the Amalekites, they were angry with David for leading them into such a predicament. His men were even talking about stoning him. So what did David do? The Bible says he *"strengthened himself in the Lord his God."* David had made some poor choices, and so have I. I've also strengthened myself in the Lord. He has rejuvenated me, restored me, calmed me, and yes, strengthened me. But that strengthening didn't happen on the run. It happened when I was still, quiet, and broken. I listen better when I'm broken, when I'm at the end of myself, when I have nowhere to turn but to the Lord. It is in those moments of waiting on the Lord that I regain strength.

Mary waited on the Lord quietly and contentedly. David strengthened himself in the Lord. Do those two actions have anything in common? You bet. There are a number of ways to strengthen yourself in the Lord, but none any better than just getting alone with Him and leaving your burden with Jesus. That's right, leave your troubles with Jesus and walk away. I found the longer I carried my burdens the heavier they became.

Jesus is my burden bearer. So my friend, strengthen yourself in the Lord, make time to do it, and do it often. Mary did, and the Lord said she had done a good thing.

MARY WEPT: JOHN 11:31-33

We don't see Martha weeping. Yet Mary is not only weeping, she is surrounded by those who are weeping with her and willing to go to the grave with her. There it is in the scriptures, *"Jesus saw her weeping."* Even though she said very little in response to Lazarus' death, her weeping speaks volumes. She wept. She mourned. She grieved.

I've wept more as a grown man than I want to admit. When I struggled to answer God's call on my life, I wept. When my mother's health was failing, I wept. I've wept over my children both tears of joy and heartache. When my marriage was ending, I wept. After it ended, I wept. Grieving and weeping is understood only by those who have grieved and wept, over circumstances they had no control over. I didn't understand the grief of losing one's parents until I lost mine. I didn't understand the grief of having a father struggle with dementia until my dad struggled. I didn't understand the absolute emptiness and grief that comes with divorce until I found myself alone. Go ahead and cry if you need to. I recommend it. In Psalm 34:18 we read, *"The Lord is near to the brokenhearted..."*

Our fast-paced society doesn't allow much time for grieving. In the United States, a person who dies on Monday will be in the grave by Wednesday. Some religious groups and family traditions may allow more time, but most of us know our funeral could be the day after tomorrow. In two days the church could be filled with mourners, the flowers displayed, and the preacher's notes prepared for your memorial service. Makes me want to make my days matter. Makes me want to live today like it's my last because I could be in Heaven by morning.

Needless to say the funeral business is a big business. In a matter of hours after a loved one dies, the family has met with the funeral home, determined a place of burial, decided on the place and time of the funeral, called the pastor and those who will sing, and bought something black to wear. And sadly, in about three days after the passing of our loved one, life goes on and we're back at work.

All that leaves little time for weeping. And surely we must understand. We've got vacations planned and ballgames to attend. We have tee times, business meetings, places to go, and people to see. We just don't have time to grieve. Besides, we've already bought the tickets to Disney, and Mother would understand. She would want us to go. *Sigh.* Yes, she would want us to go. But it's only right that we grieve.

If I may, I would like to offer a bit of advice. I think Mary would agree with me. When your loved one dies, take some time to grieve. Take a couple of days off work if you can. Stay home. Visit with family. Spend time with the Lord. Find a quiet place and seek the Lord. Let Him renew you and strengthen you. Weep. Mary did. Jesus did. You should, too.

What can we learn from these two sisters?

We can learn much from others. We can learn how we should act and react and how we shouldn't. I personally have known of a few situations when the death of a loved one divided the family more than it brought them together. Listen friends, deciding who gets the picture hanging over the mantle, Mother's piano, or Dad's truck isn't worth a family feud. May God let our loved ones rest in peace. And may God lead us to live in peace. I say that because I knew of a family a few years back that experienced the devastating loss of their father. But even more devastating was the division they experienced over what Dad had left behind. The greatest point of contention was over an acre of land on a country road, miles from town, in the middle of nowhere. The father's only real asset was this acre of land on which he lived in an older mobile home. His three children, now all in their sixties and seventies, couldn't agree with what to do with the land or what it was worth. Harsh words were spoken, legal action was taken, and a family was torn apart. All over one acre of land. Personally, peace of mind is far more valuable to me than an acre of land. May God help us.

What can we learn from Mary and Martha? **Instead of reacting with fear, respond in faith.** If you're an unbeliever or an uncommitted believer, this statement makes little sense. When the death of a friend or family member is looming or if death has actually taken place, we are often gripped by fear. We fear what we don't know and what we don't understand. May God help us. Instead of losing self-control, respond in faith. As a minister I have seen both responses. I have prayed with those who are gripped by fear. I have sensed their frustration with death and with God and with me. And I understand. I was more frustrated after my mother's passing than with my father's. My father's death was a relief. He was free from dementia. But my mother's passing caught me by surprise. I grieved, and I hurt. But I didn't grieve as though I didn't believe. Eventually I turned the corner in my grief and rested in the promise of knowing where she was.

What else can we learn? **Instead of running to the grave in confusion, run to Jesus in confidence.** I am blessed and amazed at the confidence level of many Christians. The greatest Christians never make the headlines. They live out their faith quietly and simply behind the scenes. They never wave a flag or draw attention to themselves. They have an unusual trust in God even when a dear friend or family member is about to pass away. You've heard their comments: "They're in a better place." "They're not suffering anymore." "I miss them already but I know I'll see them again someday." These words come from husbands and wives and children and parents.

I've watched in amazement as those who were facing their last days on earth grew closer to God. It seems as if their faith increased. One would think that a stage-four cancer diagnosis would create worry, fear, and anxiety. But, in many cases, I have witnessed just the opposite. I remember praying at the bedside of a godly woman who was near death. I had visited with her often and had grown to love her. As I placed my hand on her husband's shoulder, I prayed for him. I prayed for a miracle of healing in the lady who was near death, but I also prayed for this good man. *"God give him strength." "God encourage him."* When the prayer was finished, he wiped his eyes and said with confidence, *"She's in His hands."* She passed away only a few minutes later. She was in God's hands, and her husband she left behind was too.

My sweet wife Dawn lost her husband several years ago to ALS. I was friends with Arvid and had been for many years. I had visited with him occasionally when he was sick, and I was at the hospital the night he passed away. A crowd had gathered. Arvid and Dawn were much loved by their family and friends. Almost an entire city as well as many in surrounding states had prayed for him. And now he had passed. He was with the Lord. There was an unusual quietness in the hall, in the waiting room, and in the unit where he lay. Dawn and their children were there. His parents and siblings were there. His pastor and church family had come. Friends were there. And I was there because of my love for him and his family. In that quietness I felt led to lead a prayer out loud. The room was filled with hope, and confidence, and assurance. We knew where he was. He had just passed from death to life. He was immediately absent from his body but present with the Lord. I remember thanking God for the promise of eternity and the peace that comes by knowing Him. Yes, we wept but not without hope.

Martha and Mary didn't melt in a moment of confusion and unbelief. They went to Jesus in confidence. Confidence in Christ changes everything. Mary could have run to the grave, distraught over the reality of Lazarus' death. But she didn't. She went to Jesus in confidence.

We can also learn this: **Instead of criticizing Jesus for his absence, thank Him for His presence.** Most of us have been disappointed in God at some point. Of course we've been disappointed in Christians and disappointed in pastors. But some of us have been disappointed with God for not answering our prayers as we would have liked. It's easy to get critical of God and shake our fist at Him in anger. It's easy, in the heat of the moment when things don't turn out as you had thought, to take out your frustrations on God. When Martha and Mary ran to Jesus they didn't run to give Him a piece of their mind. They didn't run to demand answers. They knew if He had been there things could have turned out differently. They were glad to see Him coming.

Rest assured, you'll have a day when you'll want to give God a piece of your mind. You'll want to ask Him where He's been. You'll want to question Him about why He did what He did or why He allowed what He allowed. Maybe you're there right now. I spoke with a man recently who said he didn't think God cared about what he was going through. Well, He does. But in the moments of despair and disappointment it is hard to feel anything, even the presence of God. This man said he felt like he was alone and no one, not even God, cared. The distance we feel from God has nothing to do with God. It has everything to do with us. In the midst of your storm, take a deep breath and thank God. Find a quiet place and thank Him for everything you can think of. And in the midst of your praise, you'll discover He cares for you, loves you, and is with you. Martha and Mary could have launched into some tirade because He missed the funeral. They could have shamed Him. Instead they showed their thankfulness for His presence.

Before I finish these ideas about what we can learn from these two sisters, there's one final thing I want you to see: **It's one thing to know what you believe, but it's more important to live what you believe.** Martha and Mary knew Lazarus would live again in the resurrection. They had complete confidence that had Jesus been there Lazarus would still be alive. Martha and Mary are more than just two women in scripture who needed Jesus at a point of desperation. They are us. They believed. And they lived what they believed.

Our churches are filled with good people who know what they believe, but seldom live what they believe. If my Christian life can be defined by a once a week Sunday morning service, that says a lot about me personally, but even more about what I really believe. Here's the question we must all answer: Do I live what I believe? Again, look at what Mary did. When she rushed out of the house to go to Jesus, many of those present thought she was going to the tomb to weep. She lived according to what she believed. *"Lord if you had been here..."* was not a statement of animosity, fear, and doubt. It was a profession of faith. She believed in Jesus. And she lived like it.

I have been preaching for a number of years now. From my late teens through my twenties and thirties and forties and now in my late fifties I have preached God's goodness and faithfulness. As a young man I remember preaching funerals and trying to comfort the hurting when I had no idea what they were feeling. I had never grieved like that. I remember standing with families at gravesides quoting scripture I believed would help them in their time of need. But I didn't really know what they needed because I had never grieved like that. I remember praying with parents whose children were struggling, graduating, leaving home, and facing difficulties of their own. I remember comforting and encouraging. But I couldn't relate to them then. I had never worried like that. I remember counseling with men and women whose marriage was facing divorce. I quoted all the right verses, said all the right things, but really had no idea how they were hurting. I had never grieved like that.

Now I know. My mother and dad are in Heaven. My children are grown and pursuing their own dreams. I've been through a few storms. I've been broken, and I've been blessed. Time is a great teacher. As I've grown older I've been practicing what I've preached... *Trust the Lord. Give it to God. Don't give up. Pray. Believe. Be strong in Him. Stand on the Word. Don't be afraid. Keep your knees down and your chin up.*

Believers, we're a beautiful and sometimes unusual bunch. Folks who love Jesus are everywhere. They're realtors, farmers, doctors, lawyers, teachers, factory workers, mechanics, engineers, and the list goes on. They live in every subdivision, on every street, and on every country back road. Many of us are serious about what we believe. From grandparents to grandchildren, from seven years old to eighty-seven, we are marked by t-shirts, bumper stickers, gold crosses, WWJD bracelets, KJV and NIV Bibles. God remind us that our greatest mark is our faithfulness. While faithfulness is an easy subject to preach, it is indeed more difficult to practice. What we need is to be filled afresh and stirred anew with the promise and hope of the resurrection. Mary and

Martha would never be the same. And once we fully embrace the resurrection of Christ and of believers, we are transformed. God help us to be marked by the power of the resurrection!

Now I want to turn your attention to the believers who experienced the resurrection firsthand. What an amazing, life-changing day in the lives of those early Christians. Following the resurrection, what were the believers doing?

THEY WORSHIPPED! MATT 28:9-10

And as they went to tell His disciples, behold, Jesus met them, saying, "Rejoice!" So they came and held Him by the feet and worshipped Him. Then Jesus said to them, "Do not be afraid. Go and tell my brethren to go to Galilee, and there they will see Me."

THEIR HEARTS BURNED! LUKE 24:32-34

And they said to one another, "Did not our heart burn within us while He talked with us on the road, and while He opened the scriptures to us?" So they rose up that very hour and returned to Jerusalem, and found the eleven and those who were with them gathered together, saying, "The Lord is risen indeed…"

THEY EMBRACED HIM! JOHN 20:16-18

Jesus said to her, "Mary!" She turned and said to Him, "Rabboni!" Jesus said to her, "Do not cling to Me, for I have not yet ascended to My Father; but go to my brethren and say to them, 'I am ascending to my Father and your Father, and to my God and your God.'" Mary Magdalene came and told the disciples that she had seen the Lord, and that He had spoken these things to her.

THEY REJOICED! JOHN 20:19-20

In the evening of that first day of the week, the disciples were gathered together with the doors locked because of their fear of the Jews. Then Jesus came, stood among them, and said to them, "Peace to you!" Having said this, He showed them His hands and His side. So the disciples rejoiced when they saw the Lord.

THEY BELIEVED! JOHN 20:26-29

And after eight days His disciples were again inside, and Thomas with them. Jesus came, the doors being shut, and stood in the midst, and said, "Peace to you!" Then He said to Thomas, "Reach your finger here, and look at my hands; and reach your hand here, and put it into my side. Do not be unbelieving, but believing." And Thomas answered and said to Him, "My Lord and my God!" Jesus said to him, "Thomas, because you have seen me, you have believed. Blessed are those who have not seen and yet have believed."

ME AND MARTHA...

I am a work in progress. I am like the vessel of clay that became marred in Jeremiah 18. The Lord continues to break me and remold me. Needless to say, the Lord is still molding me to become the vessel He wants me to be. I have something in common with Martha. I have been singing her praises along with Mary's these last few chapters. But honestly, I am glad neither of them appears to be perfect. Their imperfections leave hope for me. Notice what Martha said in John 11:39. Jesus simply said, *"Take away the stone."* Martha said, *"By now he smells, for he has been dead four days."* I get the idea Martha was content to leave well enough alone and leave Lazarus in the grave. After all, it had been four days. Was Martha weak in her faith or a work in progress? Maybe a little of both.

There may be a stone in your life God wants to roll away. A big rock He wants to move. God has moved a few stones in my life even when I didn't believe as I should and when I didn't believe He could. Jesus said to Martha, "...*If you'll believe you will see the glory of God.*" God is so good. He often rolls the stone away even when we doubt He can.

Me and Martha... My prayer for me, Martha, and all of you reading these words, is that God will continue to amaze and surprise us. He still rolls away stones. May God help us believe. And when we don't believe as we should, may He help us enjoy the surprise of seeing His glory.

4

ONE HOPE

Jesus... One name. One mission. One hope.

John 12:1-2

Have you ever lost hope? Ever given up? Ever thought no one cared? Have you ever felt God had forgotten you?

....You had been sick so long, you thought you'd never get better.

....Your son or daughter had been at Children's Hospital so much the doctors and nurses knew your family on a first name basis.

....You lost your job and you lost your home and you almost lost your mind.

....You buried your wife, and you've sat for hours and talked to her picture.

....You buried your husband, and sometimes you thought you heard his voice.

....You buried your son or daughter....Or your mother or father. And you felt as if you couldn't face another day without them.

...Your husband left you and the kids and married someone else. You feel unloved and unnecessary.

...Your wife left you because she didn't love you anymore. The house is empty now, and so are you.

....Some of you have been there.

....Some of you are there now.

Is there any hope?

DOES JESUS REALLY MAKE A DIFFERENCE?

On a lighter note, isn't it odd the kind of things we let drain the hope out of us? Take, for instance, losing a ballgame. In the great state of Alabama, we believe in God, but we also believe in football. Folks in Alabama have been known to miss their daughter's wedding because of a football game. Alabama and Auburn fans are crazy. Caps and t-shirts and tattoos and insanity mark them. Auburn fans are likely to buy a blue automobile and proudly display an orange "War Eagle" tag. Alabama fans like to drive automobiles with a crimson color and then proudly display on the back glass a picture of a houndstooth hat. Here in Alabama people even name their kids and their pets after their team's coach. I'm not making that up. These same folks dedicate rooms in their homes to their team. Some of these same people, when they die, are remembered in their obituary as "someone who loved Crimson Tide football." Or "someone who loved War Eagle football."

I am telling you something you will only hear from a preacher in Alabama. If Alabama and Auburn both win on Saturday, Sunday worship attendance is much better. If either of them lose, you can sense it in the air. Ask one of those folks on Sunday morning who seem a little down, "What's wrong? What happened?" They'll simply say, *"We lost."* I'm not making this up either. If both teams win, revival is a real possibility. There seem to be more hallelujahs and amens on Sundays after an Alabama or Auburn victory on Saturday.

But if they lose... Attendance suffers. Offerings may be less. More folks get "sick" on Sunday when their team loses on Saturday. The choir is a little flat. And it's basically a day of grieving. I'm exaggerating a bit, but some of what I'm saying is true. We allow trivial things, like ballgames, to get us down. We lose hope much too easily.

The story of Lazarus, Martha, and Mary is a story of hope. It's a story of believing God and holding out hope even when there is every reason to give up. If you are at the point of giving up, I want to encourage you to hold on. Turn back to Jesus. Trust Him again. Believe in Him again.

In the days following Lazarus' resurrection, and only six days before the Passover, Jesus came to Bethany to spend a few days with some of his best friends. I have always thought these few verses at the beginning of John chapter twelve were unusual, humorous, interesting, and inspiring. First of all, imagine having Jesus over for dinner. This picture of Jesus sitting down for a meal intrigues me. It's hard for me to see Him doing that. I know He had to eat, but I get the idea He ate on the run, on His way to another city, another opportunity to teach and preach. But here He is sitting at a table where Martha is serving.

As the old saying goes, wouldn't you like to have been a fly on the wall? To see these friends together…to hear their conversation… and simply to say, "I was there." For a few brief moments, they sit and enjoy a meal together. This wasn't the *Last Supper*, but it was probably the last one they would enjoy together. Passover was six days away. And John tells us in 12:10-11, there was a plot to kill Lazarus because on his account many of the Jews believed in Jesus. Jesus was taking risks as He journeyed this close to Jerusalem, but still He knew His life was in the Father's hands. So here we find Him, relaxed and enjoying a meal with Mary, Martha, and Lazarus.

What was the talk around the table? Imagine the meal is finished and they begin to recount the events of Lazarus' sickness, death, and resurrection. Somewhere in the conversation someone must have told Martha to sit down. The dishes can wait. Imagine the tears of joy as they now realize the importance of Jesus being late. Lazarus' death was not accidental. It was on purpose that unbelievers and believers alike might see the glory of God. He had not been healed of his sickness. He had been resurrected from the dead. I imagine Mary reached over at some point and put her hand on Lazarus' hand. He was alive, and they were together once more. The least she could do was give glory to God for the miracle of saving Lazarus' life. We see her doing that in the next verses as she anoints the feet of Jesus. The atmosphere in the room was one of thanksgiving. Hope had come home.

Imagine as they talked about how they felt when Lazarus walked out of the grave. Martha must have said something like, "I couldn't believe my eyes." Lazarus must have told them what it was like hearing his name being called. Imagine Lazarus in the grave. He was absent from the body, so he must have been present with God. But Jesus called him back. Imagine that conversation. When he walked out of that grave, there must have been weeping. They must have cried for joy. But now, in the comfort of their home, they remember the miracle and can't keep their eyes off Lazarus.

While they couldn't keep their eyes off Lazarus, Jesus couldn't keep His mind off the cross. Jesus could hear the calling of the cross. He was with Martha, Mary, and Lazarus not just for a dinner, but to prepare each of them for the journey ahead. This would be some of the last fellowship He would have with them before He would go to the cross. Imagine the talk around the table. I believe there were at least three things they talked about:

THE RESURRECTION OF LAZARUS

It was the talk of the town. By now everyone had heard about Lazarus' four-day stint in the grave. He could have written a book, "96 Hours in the Grave." Today his story would have gone viral on the internet. He would have been on stage at a Franklin Graham Crusade. He could have been getting paid to tell his story. When Lazarus walked down the street people might have whispered, "Isn't that Lazarus?" Some ran to touch him, amazed that he was alive. Today he could have been a celebrity.

Elvis is dead. I was fourteen years old when he died. I was at Opryland in Nashville with a church youth group when the announcement was made over the loudspeaker that he had died. The date was August 16, 1977. I remember watching the funeral procession on TV. I remember reading the headlines in the local newspaper. I also remember reading, at different times over the past forty-plus years, of Elvis sightings. Some folks think he never died, that he's alive and well in Memphis selling hamburgers at a local McDonalds. Well, I believe he died and was buried. And I also believe Lazarus died. But Lazarus walked out of the grave. Imagine that!

When Lazarus came back to life, it had to have been almost unbelievable. But for a few who believed the scriptures and believed in Jesus, they didn't doubt it. **Lazarus' resurrection confirmed everything the scriptures predicted about Jesus.** Look at Luke 4:18-21. *"The Spirit of the Lord is upon me, because he hath anointed me to preach the gospel to the poor; he hath sent me to heal the brokenhearted, to preach deliverance to the captives, and recovering of sight to the blind, to set at liberty them that are bruised, to preach the acceptable year of the Lord. And he closed the book, and he gave it again to the minister, and sat down. And the eyes of all them that were in the synagogue were fastened on him. And he began to say unto them, "This day is this scripture fulfilled in your ears."'*

Jesus was quoting from Isaiah. Everything Jesus did was a fulfillment of Isaiah's prophecy. Lazarus was a captive to the grave while others were captives to sin. In either case, Jesus set captives free. He was not bound by people's belief or unbelief.

Think about it. Even though there was no Bible as we know it today, Isaiah was shouting from eternity, "This is Him. This is the Lord! Listen to Him." The scriptures were coming to life right before their eyes. Another thing they must have talked about was: **How the resurrection of Lazarus had created a following among the Jews.** Look at John 11:45. *"Then many of the Jews who had come to Mary, and had seen the things Jesus did, believed in Him."* Imagine the number of new believers we might have in our churches if we experienced a miracle similar to that of Lazarus' resurrection. We're no different. We seem to respond to the drastic and inconceivable. The resurrection of Lazarus today would cause people to buy into religion and come to church like they never came before. In that day Lazarus' resurrection stirred up the unbelieving Jews. They heard what Mary said and saw what Jesus did...and they believed.

The Sunday following September 11, 2001 was a day of repentance, confession of sin, and brokenness. I remember the revival meeting I preached the week following the bombing. The singing was more heartfelt. The prayers were more passionate. The sermon was easier to preach. The altar was filled. It was an amazing week. I talked with other pastors whose churches also experienced revival during those few days. But by the end of September that year most churches were back to normal. This is what we know: When Jesus went to the cross, much of the crowd that had followed Him left Him. If anyone ever told you that following Jesus is easy, they lied. Becoming a Christian is easy. Being a Christian is difficult. It means denying yourself, following the narrow way, and forgiving your enemies.

A crowd of unbelieving Jews was suddenly warming up to Jesus. He was popular. Some wanted to crown Him king. But not everyone was happy with Jesus. The religious leaders of that day saw how things were quickly getting out of hand. But what would they do? This is what we see in John's Gospel: **The resurrection of Lazarus also caused an uprising among the Pharisees.** Look at John 11:46-48. *"But some of them went away to the Pharisees and told them the things Jesus did. Then the chief priests and the Pharisees gathered a council and said, "What shall we do? For this Man works many signs. If we let Him alone like this, everyone will believe in Him."* Their power was threatened. They couldn't deny the obvious. The reasons to kill him began to outweigh the reasons not to.

Not only were average, everyday Pharisees being swayed by Jesus' miracles and His following, even some of the most recognizable names among the religious elite were beginning to believe. Remember Nicodemus? He was a Pharisee and a ruler of the Jews. Many scholars believe he was a member of the Sanhedrin, the governing body of the Jews. In our day it would be similar to his being a member of the Supreme Court. In street talk,

Nicodemus was a big shot. But after a conversation with Jesus one night, he was never the same.

John chapters three, seven, and nineteen give us glimpses into the heart of Nicodemus. After that conversation in chapter three, we see him defending Jesus' innocence in chapter seven. Then in chapter nineteen, Nicodemus and Joseph of Arimathea are making sure the body of Jesus received a proper burial. That's what we know about him. What we don't know is what had been going on in his heart and mind since that evening encounter. And we don't know how many others Jesus talked with that may have had the same reaction.

At any rate, Jews from far and wide were believing and following. On the other hand, some were also talking about crucifying Him. It had been rumored, but now specific plans were being made. Seems like the resurrection of Lazarus was a turning point. The Pharisees and chief priests had had enough. Jesus had crossed the line. He would surely die.

THE REVENGE OF THE ENEMY

Our enemy, Satan, and all those who are against Christ will fight till the end in an attempt to see Christianity snuffed out. Righteousness will always be ridiculed. Those who do right will always be wronged. But as I heard a preacher say years ago, *"The devil will turn up the heat, but God controls the thermostat."* Satan is like a dog on a leash. He's like a bird in a cage. He's like a fish in a pool. He can only go so far and do so much. I'll admit, that dog on a chain is no poodle. That bird in the cage is no songbird. And that fish in the pool is more like a piranha than a goldfish. But Satan is limited. He is not all-powerful. He is not all-knowing. Jesus is Lord and Satan is not. And since the Garden of Eden the enemy has been at work deceiving anyone he can.

What I must remember is to keep my distance from that dog on the leash. I better not let that bird out of the cage. And I should know better than to swim with a piranha. Why? Given the opportunity, Satan will attack me with the intention of destroying me. Given the opportunity, Satan will erase all that is good and bring to ruin all who follow Christ. The Enemy never sleeps.

Let's think back again to the story of Lazarus' resurrection. He had died and was buried. He had been dead four days when Jesus came back and called him by name, raised him to life, and gave a happier ending to Lazarus' story than anyone could have predicted. Good thing He called him by name or else every grave in the world would have burst open. Lazarus was alive! It was a time of celebration for his friends and family.

But it was a time of scheming for the enemies of Christ. It was then they began to carry out the plot to kill Lazarus. Look at John 12:9-11. *"Now a great many of the Jews knew that He was there; and they came, not for Jesus' sake only, but that they might also see Lazarus, whom He had raised from the dead. But the chief priests plotted to put Lazarus to death also, because on account of him many of the Jews went away and believed in Jesus."*

Mary, Martha, Lazarus, and Jesus were sitting around a table, sharing a meal and talking about what had happened the last few days and what was likely to happen the next few. No doubt they talked about the enemies of both Lazarus and Jesus. They had heard the talk. They weren't there for the food or the fellowship. They were there to talk about the future and their faithfulness to God whatever the future held.

What are you going to do if you're a Pharisee or a ruler of the Jews and one of your two greatest threats is up walking around after being dead for four days? Not only is he alive and well, but also unbelieving Jews are now believing. Lazarus is living proof of who Jesus said he was and what He said He could do. What are you going to do? They'll plan to silence him not in prison but by taking his life. Lazarus is a walking billboard advertising the power of God. Would to God our lives also tell of His might!

Have you ever wanted to kill somebody? No, ladies, I'm not talking about your husband when he forgot your anniversary. I'm talking about being so full of hatred and revenge and bitterness that you wanted to kill someone. Most of us have never been that angry. To secretly plot and plan another person's murder is something most of us will never know anything about. What does it take to be a murderer?

I found some interesting observations by Stanton Samenow. He authored the 2004 book, *Inside the Criminal Mind*. In regard to why someone decides to murder another person he says, *"There's a profound sense of powerlessness, and powerless people tend to hit back.... These are people who are already angry."* He continues, *"...and when things don't go the way they want them to, they personalize it."*

When I read those words I thought how they describe the actions of those who sought to kill Lazarus and also to crucify Jesus. Because of Jesus' overwhelming popularity and his power to raise the dead, the Pharisees began to feel their power being stripped away. If powerless people tend to hit back, the angry Jews were going to hit Lazarus. They felt personally offended. Their power and prestige was being jeopardized. They were offended. Add that to the anger they already felt toward Christ and the decision to take the life of Lazarus was their only choice.

Never forget, the same spirit that caused people to hate Christ two thousand years ago still causes people to hate Christians today. Just recently while watching a protest against racial injustice, I saw a man carrying a sign that said, *"If Jesus comes back kill Him again."* As if Jesus was racially unjust. He was the most racially reconciling person who ever walked the earth. But He also exposed the hypocrisy of the Jews. And they hated Him for it. They hated Him even more for raising Lazarus. He's still hated today because He stands for everything the world is against. And when faced with the truth of His words, the world also feels powerless.

Before I dive into the next idea, I want to give you a minute to absorb that last paragraph. We cannot imagine the hatred many of the Jews, the religious leaders, and Pharisees had toward Jesus. They wished they had never heard His name. As much as believers loved Him, the unbelieving Jews hated Him. Wow! Think about that. And after you've pondered the depth of their hatred, think about what Billy Graham said, *"If Jesus were to come today just as He did 2000 years ago, He would be crucified in less time than He was then."* The goal then was to kill Jesus. And to silence His followers. Has anything changed?

Look at John 11:53-57. *"Then, from that day on, they plotted to put Him to death. Therefore Jesus no longer walked openly among the Jews, but went from there into the country near the wilderness, to a city called Ephraim, and there remained with His disciples. And the Passover of the Jews was near, and many went from the country up to Jerusalem before the Passover, to purify themselves. Then they sought Jesus, and spoke among themselves as they stood in the temple, 'What do you think — that He will not come to the feast?' Now both the chief priests and the Pharisees had given a command, that if anyone knew where He was, he should report it, that they might seize Him."*

They *"plotted to put Him to death,"* thus taking away the hope of these soon to be Christians. They intended to literally kill their joy. They would murder their king. Their plan was never just to seize Him, but to crucify Him. Nothing has really changed. The silence of Christians would be a pleasing sound to the ears of Satan. But in the story of Lazarus the Pharisees didn't want just silence, they wanted Jesus to be silenced. Little did they realize their attempt to quiet Him would awaken a message that still rings today. Messengers have been silenced, but the message still shouts His grace, His power, and His coming! Oh, the power of the Gospel!

If believers are to make a difference for Christ and fulfill the Great Commission, we cannot be silent. While the enemy would like for us to purr like kittens, we must continue to roar like lions. Not in arrogance and pride, but in confidence and with compassion. It is the power of the Gospel that does the work.

Following Lazarus' resurrection, the enemy's revenge was stoked. Like a raging fire, Lazarus' death and resurrection had been like throwing fuel on the fire. They plotted to kill Lazarus. Their priority was to kill Jesus. They were in league with Satan whose priority was to deceive believers. Look at John 10:7-11. *"Then Jesus said to them again, "Most assuredly, I say to you, I am the door of the sheep. All who ever came before Me are thieves and robbers, but the sheep did not hear them. I am the door. If anyone enters by Me, he will be saved, and will go in and out and find pasture. The thief does not come except to steal, and to kill, and to destroy. I have come that they may have life, and that they may have it more abundantly. I am the good shepherd. The good shepherd gives His life for the sheep."*

Long before Lazarus died and rose again, Jesus knew and warned believers of what the devil came to do. Satan is described as a thief. Thieves are known for one thing: stealing. Satan is a thief. What does he plan on stealing? He wants to steal the glory that belongs to God. He wants to steal the innocence of children. He wants to take away marriages and rob families and steal homes. He wants to steal the futures of high school and college students. He wants to steal fellowship from churches. He wants to take away our Bibles. He wants to rob us of our freedom to pray. He is a thief and he has only one thing in mind: steal everything that matters. Steal, kill, and destroy. And he is good at what he does.

We are living in unprecedented times. 2020 opened our eyes to the insanity of evil and the power of the unbelieving world against Christians. Christians have even been described as a hate group. That was in response to what the Bible says about marriage being between a man and a woman. Hatred for the church has always existed, but we may see more hostility in the days to come. 2 Timothy 3 reminds us in the last days perilous times will come. *"Men will be lovers of themselves..."* We have seen those verses coming to life right before our eyes. May the Lord strengthen His church to stand with courage, boldness, compassion, and faithfulness.

In Genesis chapter 3 the serpent is described as being *"...more cunning than any creature the Lord God made."* Satan is the best when it comes to deception. There has never been another like him. In Genesis 3:1 he initiated a conversation with Eve. *"Has God said you cannot eat of every tree of the garden?"* Eve responded, *"We can eat of the trees of the garden except the tree which is in the midst of the garden. If we even touch it, we will die."* Satan replied, *"You won't die. God knows when you eat of that fruit you will be like Him."* Did you notice what happened? The serpent spoke. Eve spoke. But God has already spoken. Both the serpent and Eve knew what God had said, but the serpent causes Eve to doubt God's words.

Since the beginning of time, Satan has been causing people to doubt what God has said. When God speaks, whatever He says is truth. God's word is truth. His words are absolute truths. Times change, but God's word never changes. People change, but God's word remains the same. People riding in a horse and buggy once traveled the road in front of my home. Over time we have witnessed amazing progress. We now have automobiles that can almost drive themselves. In a world so full of changes and forward progress in travel and technology, rest assured God's word hasn't changed one bit. What was true when Jesus said it is still true today.

Charles Swindoll tells an amazing story of a community that formed in the aftermath of the *Mutiny on the Bounty*. Although much of the information that follows was gleaned from Wikipedia.com and SermonCentral.com, it is Charles Swindoll's enthusiastic delivery and interesting details that inspire me to share the story with you. It's worth repeating. The *Bounty* was a ship. The mutiny occurred after the captain of the ship, William Bligh, enforced serious punishment on his crew.

The *Bounty* set sail from Portsmouth, England on December 23, 1787 on a mission to gather fruit trees from Polynesia and transport them to the British West Indies. The journey was a long one, ten months and twenty-seven thousand miles. They remained in Tahiti gathering breadfruit trees for well over a year. During this time the crew of the ship developed relationships with the local women and some even married. When it came time to leave the island, they had difficult separating themselves from the life they had grown accustomed to. They were commanded to leave their wives and the relationships they had established, board the *Bounty*, and head back home. This would lead to the eventual mutiny on the *Bounty*.

Following the mutiny with numerous fights and disagreements, the captain and eighteen crew members, loyal to their mission, set sail and eventually arrived in Indonesia. The leader of the mutiny, Fletcher Christian, and several men returned to the island. They went back to get their wives and along the way freed themselves of unwanted baggage, sixteen men who did not want to continue the mutiny. They eventually landed on Pitcairn Island, an isolated place where they could hide and enjoy the lifestyle they had chosen. However after years of alcohol abuse and fighting over the women, only two of the original mutineers remained, John Adams and Ned Young.

Six years later Young died of asthma, and Adams was left with eleven women and twenty-three children. At some point Adams had a change of heart. He turned his attention to a Bible they had taken from the *Bounty*. He repented and began to lead a new life based on the teachings of the Bible. With the Bible as his guide, he educated the children, built a school, and created a way of life based on the teachings of the scriptures. Later Adams wrote, *"I had been working like a mole for years, and suddenly it was as if the doors were flung wide open, and I saw the light, and I met God in Jesus Christ. And the burden of my sin rolled away, and I found new life in Christ."* In 1808 the island of Pitcairn was rediscovered by Americans, and then again in 1814 by the British. Those who rediscovered the island were amazed and impressed by the character of the residents.

Character. Where do you think that "character" came from? No doubt it was the result of the power of God's word that had transformed a man and then a community. Never underestimate the power of God's word. Friend, you may become discouraged, even depressed about your circumstances, but be careful that you don't become deceived. God's word is truth. And His truth makes us free.

THE REDEMPTION OF THE WORLD

Think about these words: God's purposes have always been redemptive. That's an idea I have been preaching for many years. From the Garden of Eden, where an animal was killed so the skin could be used to cover the nakedness of Adam and Eve, to the cross of Christ where the blood He shed would be used to cover the sins of all who would ever believe, God has had redemption in mind. When He was on the cross, redemption was on His mind. Look at this great and often overlooked passage of scripture about Christ's death: John 11:50-51 *"...Nor do you consider that it is expedient for us that one man should die for the people, and not that the whole nation should perish." Now this he did not say on his own authority; but being high priest that year he prophesied that Jesus would die for the nation."*

In saying these words, Caiphas had no intention of quoting scripture or giving a prophecy that would be fulfilled. He was being rational. He was giving a good and sensible reason why it would be better for Jesus to die. Adam Clarke says, *"He had no other intention than merely to state that it was better to put Jesus to death than to put the whole nation in jeopardy on his account."* In other words, it was better to sacrifice one man than a whole nation.

Like it or not, Caiphas and a host of others found themselves right in the middle of scripture being fulfilled—and written. They had no idea two thousand years from then that we would be reading the account of Jesus' death, burial, and resurrection. They had no way of knowing they were a part of the greatest event in the history of the world. They didn't know, but God did. And everything that happened was according to His will.

When Mary, Martha, Lazarus, and Jesus sat around that table sharing a meal just six days before Passover, I believe they talked about the resurrection of Lazarus, the revenge of the enemy, and last but not least, the redemption of the world. Jesus knew. Lazarus, Mary, and Martha had heard enough that they should have had an idea about what was coming. In John 12:23 Jesus spoke clearly, *"The hour has come that the Son of Man should be glorified."*

Why did Jesus go to the cross? John 3:16 says, *"God so loved the world that He gave his only Son."* Jesus went to the cross to save, to redeem, and most of all to please the Heavenly Father. And because He went, whosoever believes in Jesus can be saved. Forever…never to be lost again.

We were there when they crucified our Lord

Do you remember the words to the old spiritual, *"Were you there?"*
The words are penetrating, convicting, and heart rending.

"Were you there when they crucified my Lord?

Were you there when they crucified my Lord?

O sometimes it causes me to tremble, tremble, tremble.

Were you there when they crucified my Lord?"

The truth is, we were there. We were there shouting,
"Crucify Him!" We were the soldiers. We were the crowd mocking
His name. We were the disciples who turned back in unbelief. We
were the men at the foot of the cross gambling for His clothes.

Were we there? Yes, we were. We tasted the wine at the
marriage…we were the crippled who stood and walked…we
were the blind who saw…the deaf who heard…the dumb who
spoke…the dead who were resurrected…the rejected who were
accepted…and the hated who were loved. The One who so loved
the world was so rejected by those who knew Him best.

Were we there when they crucified our Lord? Yes. But the good
news of the Gospel is that Jesus was there. Because He was there,
we have hope. Hope that shines in the midst of despair. Hope
that sings in the midst of sorrow.

**We have hope because Jesus loved people no one else
would love.** Look at John 8:7-12. Jesus never practiced selective
evangelism. We tend to reach out to those who look like us, act
like us, and agree with us. But Jesus didn't ignore anyone for any
reason. He loved the rich. He loved the poor. He loved the
influential. He loved the outcast. He loved those who loved Him.
He loved those who hated Him. He sat on a well by a Samaritan

woman who had been married five times, he ate at the home of a tax collector, he forgave a woman caught in the act of adultery, and he became friends with a man who had been demon-possessed, naked, and living in the tombs. The religious establishment didn't know what to do with Him.

What about this woman caught in the act of adultery? She didn't deny her sin. She did it. But what would Jesus do? What would He say? Would He stone her according to the law? Jesus told the stone casters to cast their stones only if they had no sin. They all walked away. Jesus loved people no one else would love. But some are still picking up stones today, eager to cast at some poor soul bound by the Devil and ostracized by believers. Jesus was never easy on sin. But he was even harder on hypocrites who could quote scripture but knew nothing about grace.

What about lepers who were cast out by government, religion and society? They were sick, suffering, and shoved outside the city limits. The lepers of that day represent more than people with a disease. They are a picture of all those outside the church, grace, and forgiveness, who have no hope of ever being loved and accepted.

Leprosy was a contagious disease. Treatment was limited if it existed at all. Colonies were necessary for the health of the majority. The problem in scripture, however, was not the disease but the attitude of the Pharisees toward those who had the disease. Then came Jesus who loved even lepers. Jesus loved people no one else would love.

What about a disciple named Judas who was captivated by the enemy? Did Jesus love him? Absolutely. On the night of his betrayal and arrest, Jesus looked into the eyes of Judas and asked, *"Friend, why have you come?"* Jesus knew why he had come, but He gave Judas an opportunity to back out of his deal with the enemy. He could have cried out, "Forgive me!" and Jesus would have forgiven him. But instead of running to Jesus he ran to the enemy. Jesus loved the one who betrayed him. And because of that wonderful story and countless others in scripture, I know there is hope for me and anyone who will believe. Jesus loved people no one else would love.

We have hope because Jesus went places no one else would go. I'm sure you've passed through small towns and big cities before when you've thought, "How could anyone live here?" The sight of dilapidated homes, wrecked cars, and tires for flower pots (only in Alabama) made you want to put the pedal to the metal and get out of town quick. You might have even mused, "I didn't realize there were places like this in the United Sates."

One day Jesus went to a condemned city called Jericho. Remember Jericho? If you're my age and you ever attended Vacation Bible School as a child you might remember the song about Joshua marching seven times around, *"And the walls came tumbling down…"* Remember that? The story is found in Joshua chapter 6. The children of Israel marched around Jericho once a day for six days. On the seventh day they marched around the city seven times. On the seventh time around the trumpets were to blow, the ram's horn was to sound, and the people were to shout. They did, and the walls came down. In Joshua 6:26, the Lord commanded that no man rebuild the walls of Jericho. The city was destroyed to never be rebuilt. Pretty interesting considering that in Luke chapter nineteen Jesus entered and passed through Jericho. To make a long story short, while He was there Zacchaeus became a follower of Christ. It's an amazing story to say the least. But greatest of all we see Jesus going to a condemned city to reach condemned people. Before you write a place off as being unreachable, talk to Jesus about it.

One day Jesus went through Samaria. In John chapter four the Bible says, *"It was necessary…"* While passing through Samaria, Jesus came to a place called Sychar. Samaritans had been despised since the Assyrian domination back around 722 BC. Racial slurs were common when Jews spoke of the Samaritans. While there Jesus met a woman of Samaria who had been married five times and was living with another man at the time. While sitting at Jacob's well, He offered her living water. A while later she got a taste of what Jesus was talking about, and her life was immediately changed.

Samaria and the Samaritan woman…who would have thought it? Not only was she a sinner, she was a Samaritan, and she was a woman. Three strikes against any Jew claiming to be a religious leader sitting and talking to a person such as she was. What's He doing associating with her kind? Jesus went to a place with a history to reach a woman with a history. Jesus went places no one else would go.

One day Jesus went to Golgotha. It was known as the place of the skull. We read the account of this place in Matthew 27:33, Mark 15:22, and John 19:17. It was the place where Jesus was crucified just outside the city walls of Jerusalem. It was in that place that Jesus died for the sins of all who would ever believe. It was there that an innocent Savior gave His life for guilty sinners. Why? Because God so loved the world.

The *place* was Golgotha. The *people* were all those who would ever believe in His death, burial, resurrection, and coming again. Simply put, Jesus went to a place like Golgotha to save a person like me. Jesus went places no one else could go or would go. Thank you, Jesus, for going to the cross.

We have hope because Jesus said things no one else would say. Look at John 7:45-48. John the Baptist was bold, but he never said things like Jesus said. Jesus had nothing to lose.

He could speak without fear. He was on Heaven's clock. He was in the Father's will. He was bound for the cross. The critics were dumbfounded. They said, *"No man ever spoke like this man!"* He spoke with courage and compassion. He spoke with humility and honesty. He condemned sin and loved sinners.

Jesus said His church would never be defeated. Jesus said in Matthew 16:18, *"I will build my church and the gates of Hell will not prevail against it."* The imagery here is not that of the church being attacked by the gates of Hell. But that the church is going out into all the world and the gates of Hell yielding to the power of Christ, His church, and His kingdom.

Jesus said the Devil is a murderer. In John 8:44 He said the devil *"...was a murderer from the beginning."* The prophets never said anything like this. From the time Jesus was tempted in the wilderness to His betrayal in the garden, Jesus said things no one expected Him to say. He never failed to speak the truth about Satan. He is an accuser...he is the adversary...he is the enemy... he is a liar and a murderer. No one ever said that before. Jesus said things no one else would say.

Jesus said the truth would make you free. In John 8:32 He told Abraham's descendants who didn't believe they had ever been in bondage to anyone, *"You will be made free."* Jesus was very blunt and to the point about what would destroy you, but also about what would make you free. Jesus knew who He was and what He came to do. He knew His time was limited, so He spoke with no uncertainty. Jesus was the Truth and He was going to the cross to make captives free. Whosoever believes can be made free. No one else ever said that before.

We have hope because Jesus did things no one else could do. Look at Mark 2:5-12. Jesus was forgiving sins and changing lives. He was absolutely amazing. Multitudes followed Him wherever He went. Thousands were fed with the lunch belonging to a little boy. Two thousand years later people still stand in awe of who He is and what He does. We still stand amazed in His presence.

Jesus forgave sin. Many of us who have been in church most of our life take this one lightly. The woman caught in adultery didn't take this for granted. The Samaritan woman didn't take it lightly. Don't ever forget it. When God forgives your sin, He forgets it. He will never bring it up again. For the believer, you will never have to live under the guilt of your sins. Your sins are forgiven…forgotten…forever.

Jesus healed the sick. We're still a little suspicious of this one today. But let's ask the paralytic. Better ask the leper. Ask the blind man who now sees, the deaf man who now hears. He is still the healer. When any healing comes, it comes by the hand of God. Miracles are not a thing of the past. Healing is in the hands of God and He has never changed. Jesus does things no one else can do.

Jesus promised salvation for all who would believe. In John 6:37 He said, *"The one who comes to me I will by no means cast out."* Friend, that is what many of us believe to be eternal security. Jesus will in no wise cast out those who come to Him for salvation. The Pharisees were good at casting out the ungodly and disobedient. They were known for crucifying the worst of sinners. Jesus was known for saving and redeeming the worst of sinners. The words of an old Squire Parsons song says, *"When I could not come to Him, He came to me."* Jesus loved the unlovable and saved the unsavable. And He still does. He didn't come to condemn sinners but to save them.

Jesus was born to die. He died to save. Jesus was tempted in all the ways we are, yet He never sinned. He had no sin debt. He had never fallen short of the glory of God. He didn't just "die" but suffered "death on a cross." And this followed his humiliation, his beating and scourging, and carrying of His own cross. He cried out to His Father who had forsaken Him. Look at the cross! What happened there will never be reversed. Because He died we can live. He became guilty that we could be made innocent. His death and resurrection purchased our redemption! Jesus alone is our hope.

One of my favorite stories is that of D. L. Moody as he thought about passing from this life into eternity. Moody said to a friend, *"Someday you will read in the papers that D. L. Moody is dead. Don't you believe a word of it. At that moment I shall be more alive than I am now. I shall have gone higher, that is all - out of this old clay tenement into a house that is immortal, a body that sin cannot touch, that sin cannot taint, a body fashioned into his glorious body. I was born in the flesh in 1837, was born of the Spirit in 1856. That which is born of the flesh may die. That which is born of the spirit will live forever."* Amen.

Four Days – Amazing.
Three Words – Wonderful.
Two Sisters – Inspiring.
One Hope – Eternal.

Keeping Hope Alive

5

REST IN HIM

Hebrews 4:9-11

Hoping means resting – Resting in the Lord and in His promises. But we live in a culture that doesn't encourage rest. We work hard and play hard. We're either tired, or we were tired, or we're going to be tired. From the minute our children learn to walk they are expected to run. We go until we collapse and then sleep too little before we rise to go again. Vacations have become anything but a time of rest. Many of us come home from vacation more tired than we were before we left. Weekends have become two days of cramming in everything possible including ballgames, concerts, and travel. We're often so busy on the weekend that we have no time left for church. And if we do have time we often arrive late and leave in a hurry. Summer break for our children, at one time, was actually a break, but even it has become a few weeks of hurrying to and from practices and camps. People are tired. Just look at us. Living in fast forward, running behind, and running on empty.

From the scripture in Hebrews we are allowed and even encouraged to rest. When I think of rest I think of the Sabbath. The people of God were told to remember the Sabbath and keep it holy. But we don't worship on the Sabbath, we worship on the Lord's Day or resurrection day. We are New Testament Christians and now Jesus has become our Sabbath. He is our rest. He is our comfort. He is our refuge. Since we can't do enough good works to be saved, we rest in Him who did. We can't do enough good works and great works to make ourselves more acceptable to God. We are accepted through Christ. We are saved through Christ. We rest in him. We take a wonderful deep breath knowing He did all that was necessary to save us, and now our only response is to trust Him. That gives us hope. That restores our hope.

Since I mentioned it, maybe we need to take a deep breath. Maybe right now is a good time. Maybe we need to say "No" to a few invitations and opportunities and spend a weekend at home with our family. Grill a burger. Enjoy a cup of coffee or a glass of iced tea. Enjoy a movie at home. Read a book. Talk to your kids. Call your parents. Stay at home on a Saturday and refuse to leave the house. You might find you like it. Maybe we need to find a quiet spot and listen to God. Maybe we need to spend an hour or so in prayer – eyes wide open, knocking, seeking, asking. Maybe we need to open the scriptures and rest in His promises.

I was raised at a slower pace than most kids my age. I lived just off a narrow country road surrounded by cotton fields and cattle. From mid-March to late October the sounds of planting and harvesting filled the air. As a kid I rode my bicycle, climbed trees, and explored the hills around our home. The TV had three good channels, and all that was on during the day was soap operas. Mother cleaned house, cooked meals, and washed clothes. She seldom went anywhere other than "town" to get groceries. My dad worked as a painter and builder. He came home tired, sat down for supper, and then either worked in the garden or sat on the porch. Weekends for us involved working around the house on Saturday and going to church on Sunday. Boring? If it was at the time, I didn't know it. I knew nothing about shopping malls and nice restaurants. When we shopped it was at Sears and Big K. When we ate out it was at Kentucky Fried Chicken or Burger Chef. Neither did I know much about about Vietnam and Watergate. We were cutting watermelons beneath the mulberry trees and making homemade ice cream on the back porch. Little did I know at the time how sheltered my life was. It was a slow, steady pace with a red brick church, a country store, and a home that was a safe haven. I was loved, blessed, and cared for. What more could I ask for?

A country song from several years back says, *"...things get complicated when you get past eighteen."* Yes they do. I think it's because at the time that song was popular, eighteen-year-old kids were leaving home to go to school, get married, go to work, to be on their own. And suddenly, for that young man or lady, their eyes are opened to see how mean the world can be. I would guess if that song were sung today it might be, *"...things get complicated when you get past twelve..."* Because of the internet, smartphones, and cable TV, our children are exposed to so much evil. It's difficult to raise a child in a sheltered environment anymore. I remember in my late teens and early twenties learning so much so quickly. Things like, watch your back. Be careful who you trust. If it sounds too good to be true, it is. Why is it so complicated to grow up and live in this world? Because we are continually being jerked from what we hope to what we know. From innocence to indecency. From respectable to rude. From hand shaking to back stabbing. It's complicated because it's sudden reality.

What does the rudeness of the world have to do with resting in the Lord? Everything. He is my resting place. He is my refuge. He is where I take a deep breath. He is my place of refocusing. He is the one who revives me and restores me. Better than an easy chair, better than a back porch swing, better than a beach chair with an umbrella, He is my rest.

6

REDEEM THE DAYS

Ephesians 5:15-18

I often use the word "blur" to describe the passing of time. I have used it so much some of my family wants me to stop. But I will use it here, and you can read it once and turn the page. Life is a blur. I remember when our children were being born someone told me to love them because they'd be grown before I knew what was happening. I didn't believe him. But he was right. They're all twenty-something and I am now twenty-something years older. It has been a blur. It seems that high school reunions are happening every six months. My friends are getting older quicker. Christmas comes twice a year.

My friend, Veazy Jackson, was getting a new roof put on his home a few years ago. The roofer asked him if he wanted the thirty-year shingle or the fifteen-year year shingle. He said, *"At my age I better go with the fifteen-year."* I always thought that was funny. But Veazy, who at the time was almost eighty years old, knew the shingles would probably outlive him. He was right. Life is a blur.

The scripture from Ephesians reminds us to make the most of each day. *"See then that you walk circumspectly, not as fools but as wise, redeeming the time, because the days are evil. Therefore do not be unwise, but understand what the will of the Lord is."* Redeeming the days helps build my hope in Christ. When I look back and see that I have wasted time, I am quickly discouraged. But redeeming the days encourages me and strengthens me. Time is passing quickly regardless of how I spend it, but if I spend it serving the Lord and doing what honors Him, it is time well spent. James 4:14 describes our time on earth like a vapor, a mist, or a fog that quickly vanishes. As my number of birthdays continues to increase, I see more and more what James meant. In a blink we go from having our life ahead of us to having most of it behind us. We quickly go from looking ahead to looking back. May God help guard against simply enduring our days, but rather enjoying our days.

And since life is such a blur there are a few simple things I must do. I need to get right with the Lord. I need to get right with my family, friends, and neighbors. I need to apologize if necessary, forgive if I haven't already, and tell those nearest me how much I love them. I recommend that if you're in your seventies or eighties, but I also believe it's the right thing to do if you're in your twenties or thirties. Either way, getting right with God and the people around you makes living easier. If I am right with God and my neighbor, then I am ready to die. And if I happen to live another forty years, I am good either way. I can enjoy Heaven if I go there soon, or I can enjoy life here on earth if He lets me stay a while.

As I type these words we are in the midst of a pandemic. Covid 19 is wreaking havoc across the world. As a result here in America we are seeing businesses close, schools delayed, churches struggling, sickness, and death. At the same time, we are once again seeing a rise in racial unrest. As a result of that we are seeing protests, riots, looting, and desecration of property. At the same time we are also in the midst of a presidential election crisis, a heated election process. As a result of that we are seeing a stalemate of powers among Republicans and Democrats that seem reluctant to do anything beneficial. We are also witnessing a crisis among all races, all ages, of all backgrounds creating anxiety, fear, and worry. It is a time like most of us have never seen. If ever we needed to heed the words of James, we certainly do now. Redeem the days...Rescue the days. Make the most of these days.

Our days are important and people are important, too. As I type these words I am reminded of a family who lost their home to a fire, and in that fire a wife lost her husband and children lost their dad. I think about the father and husband who has recently been diagnosed with lymphoma. A young mother comes to mind that is battling breast cancer again. I think also about the amazing couple that recently buried their child. I visited my friend recently who has suffered a stroke and now struggles to walk. I'm reminded of a dear lady who lost her husband after seventy years of marriage. I could go on. If we haven't been in a crisis in our family and with our health, there may come a day when we will. If and when that happens we have one Hope - Christ.

Keep your hope in Christ alone. Whether it is the pandemic of 2020 or the great depression of the 1920s, none of it has taken God by surprise. His grace is more than enough. He is good even in bad times. Lean on Him. Lean into Him. Learn from Him. Take a deep breath. Redeem the days.

7

ENDURE HARDSHIPS

2 Timothy 2:3-4

Angela Duckworth writes in her book *Grit, "Enthusiasm is common, endurance is rare."* She goes on to say *"Endurance is messy."* I would agree. It is messy because of the struggles, setbacks, criticism, hard days, and long nights. When I set out on this journey of being a preacher of the Gospel some thirty-eight years ago, I can tell you with all honesty I never imagined the messiness of the ministry. I was filled with enthusiasm. I was encouraged by friends. I was going to be a preacher. And now I have been one for many years, and I can tell you first hand, endurance is messy. How so? When I began in the ministry there were several young guys my age doing the same thing. Most of them are no longer in the ministry for one reason or another. Many of the churches where I have preached revival meetings are now either empty or struggling. Many of the pastors I have preached for over the years have gotten out of the ministry because of bad choices or compromised values. I have been the victim of praise and criticism, both of which will destroy a preacher if he believes either one. I have been wanted and unwanted. I have preached to packed houses, and I have preached to almost empty ones. I have survived complaints from liberals, conservatives, and fundamentalists. I have survived being corrected by both Calvinists and Armenians. I have been criticized for being too old school and judged for being too contemporary. I have survived being divorced and criticized as disqualified. But I have also been very blessed. I have endured hardships in the ministry. But I have enjoyed more mountaintops than I have endured valleys. I've enjoyed more sunshine than I've endured rain. I've laughed more than I've cried. At this point if I had it to do all over again, I'd do it in a heartbeat. I've endured hardships, but I have so enjoyed the journey.

Imagine Paul's voice as he says, *"You therefore must endure hardship as a good soldier of Jesus Christ. No one engaged in warfare entangles himself with the affairs of this life, that he may please him who enlisted him as a soldier."* The old preacher, Paul, is encouraging the young preacher, Timothy, to guard against becoming entangled in the affairs of this world. Why? I think it's because Paul knew the world will drain the hope right out of your soul. The world promises clear waters and blue skies but delivers a murky swamp and storm clouds. Paul knew it wouldn't be easy because of his own experiences. He was enduring prison when he wrote these words. Enduring hardships is a daily commitment to staying untangled with the affairs of this world.

I have been blessed in more ways than I can remember. I have endured by the grace of God. The church I was raised in has stood with me and behind me in all the changes and challenges I have faced. The first church I pastored has been like a family to me, loving me and cheering me as I have served. In each of the other two churches I pastored, there were loving, kind, and gracious people who prayed for me, encouraged me, and believed in me. I have been a member of the same church, Trinity Baptist, for almost thirty years. They have proven to be a safe haven for me and my family, as well as a place of refreshing and renewing. They have consistently blessed me, helped sustain me, and befriended me in countless ways.

I know God is the one who provides, but often He uses people. Having preached in hundreds of churches, I have never failed to receive some kind of honorarium or love offering. Sometimes it was small or slow in arriving, but I have never received nothing. I have met so many good people that I call friends who write, call, or text on a regular basis. I am friends with pastors of both large and small churches. There are good men everywhere pastoring faithfully, never making the headlines, and never gracing the conference stage, but faithful nonetheless. For every church that disqualified me because of my divorce, many others have opened their doors and allowed God to use me in their pulpits. I am blessed. I have no complaints. I have endured thus far, and I am both humbled and grateful. I hope to finish strong.

Yes, as Angela Duckworth said, *"Enthusiasm is easy, endurance is rare."* Whether you're starting a new business, a new church, a new job, getting married, or just got saved, enthusiasm is common and expected. But to endure the hardships and difficulties of growing a business, building a church, working for years at one job, staying married, or being faithful, is rare to say the least.

There is hope in the enduring. And I see no conflict between resting and enduring. In fact I believe resting in the Lord enables us to endure. Resting in Him strengthens me. The more I grow as a believer I find that I accomplish so much more if I am committed to the enduring, pursuing, believing, pressing toward the goal. I have found that the past is a good predictor of the future. As I endure hardships now, I am empowered to face hardships that are yet to come. I have confidence for the future because of the past. I look back and see the hand of God and that enables me to look forward to endure even though I can't see what lies ahead. Endure, press on, stay the course, be faithful, and be a good soldier. Put your confidence in Jesus who has already won the battle for you.

8

SING A NEW SONG

Psalm 149:1-6

"Praise the Lord! Sing to the Lord a new song, And His praise in the assembly of saints. Let Israel rejoice in their Maker; Let the children of Zion be joyful in their King. Let them praise His name with the dance; Let them sing praises to Him with the timbrel and harp. For the Lord takes pleasure in His people; He will beautify the humble with salvation. Let the saints be joyful in glory; Let them sing aloud on their beds. Let the high praises of God be in their mouth..."

Go ahead and give it a try. Not much of a singer? Doesn't matter if you can carry a tune or not. You're singing for an audience of one, the Lord Himself. Sing to Him. Sing for Him. Sing about Him. I am reminded of what my friend, Bob Pitman, said about singing. He said, *"We don't sing because we can sing, but because we have a song."* Isn't that a great idea? I want to encourage you to be hopeful and sing. It's not necessary that you know all the words, just sing the ones you know and hum the rest. You're not singing because you have a beautiful voice, you're singing because you have a voice. You're not singing because you have a perfect life, you're singing because you have a life. I suppose I must quote Buddy from the movie *Elf* who said, *"The best way to spread Christmas cheer is singing loud for all to hear."* Friend, regardless of the season of the year or the season of your life, singing just makes things better. Sing for joy. Sing for hope.

Singing has always been a happy place for me. It's been a gift I have thoroughly enjoyed for most of my life. I sang in church as a boy, and as I grew I led the singing when we met on Sunday nights and eventually Sunday mornings. Right after graduating from high school I was a part of a Gospel quartet. We were all about the same age traveling far and wide on the weekends singing anywhere we were given an opportunity. We thought we might get famous one day. We never even came close to being famous, but we sure had a good time. Those were great days and now great memories. We would load up, all six of us in two cars. We had all our equipment packed into a homemade trailer that looked like a renovated horse hauler. We called ourselves the Country Brothers because we were all from the country and we were brothers in Christ. We sang in Baptist churches, Methodist churches, Church Of God, Presbyterian, non-denominational, and just about any other church you can think of. I discovered that, regardless of our differences in beliefs, Christian music has a way of uniting all believers. We didn't know it back then, but we were having the time of our lives.

I play the guitar and piano at home. I play at home because no one would ever want to hear me play in public. I play and sing and make up songs as I go. I find real joy in doing that. It's hard for me to be sad and sing. Singing makes me hopeful and happy. Singing dries my tears. I've sung when I was hurting, worried, and fearful. But singing has a way of breaking down walls of hurt and heartache. When His praises are in my mouth, it's hard for fear to be in my heart. I'd like to share one of my favorite songs:

"IT IS WELL" BY HORATIO SPAFFORD

When peace like a river attendeth my way, when
    sorrows like sea billows roll,
Whatever my lot, Thou hast taught me to say, it is
    well, it is well with my soul.

It is well with my soul, it is well with my soul.
It is well, it is well with my soul.

Though Satan should buffet, though trials should
    come, let this blest assurance control,
That Christ has regarded my helpless estate, and
    has shed His own blood for my soul.

It is well with my soul, it is well with my soul.
It is well, it is well with my soul.

My sin, oh the bliss of this glorious thought, my
    sin, not in part, but the whole,
Is nailed to the cross, and I bear it no more, praise
    the Lord, praise the Lord, O my soul.

It is well with my soul, it is well with my soul.
It is well, it is well with my soul.

You can't be hopeless and praise the Lord at the same time. Rest
in Him! Sing a new song of hope! Sing a new song of joy. Sing a
new song of confidence in the Lord! Let the praise of God be in
your mouth!

9

TRUST GOD IN ALL THINGS

Psalm 20:7

"Some trust in chariots, and some in horses; But we will remember the name of the Lord our God."

I'm sure you remember the words to this old hymn: *"Tis so sweet to trust in Jesus, just to take Him at His word. Just to rest upon His promise, just to know thus saith the Lord."* Back in 2015 I had to practice what I had preached. It's not that I was living contrary to what I believed. It was simply that I had to trust the Lord like I had told other people to trust Him. I found it is much easier to preach a sermon than live it.

In the fall of that year, I received the divorce papers in the mail. I didn't want the divorce. I prayed it wouldn't happen. I believed God for a miracle. In spite of all that I hoped for, I was being divorced. Also at that time my father was in the early stages of dementia. He would soon leave his home and be placed in a nursing facility. It was a sad time for my dad and all of us who love him. It was a tough time for me. My preaching ministry began taking some hits as talk of the divorce began to circulate. I was forced to have conversations I didn't want to have. What was I to do while my marriage was ending, my father was weakening, and my ministry was struggling? I decided I had two choices: I could trust the Lord...or I could not trust the Lord. It was that clear.

I remember reminding myself of all I believed about God's faithfulness and goodness. I remember reminding myself of all the verses I had used as a minister to encourage others who were going through a storm. I reminded myself how God had never failed me. I had never missed a meal, a car payment, a mortgage payment, and had never gone without a place to preach since I surrendered to the ministry. I knew I could trust Him. He had been faithful. And now I sensed an obligation to be faithful to Him.

I want to tell you how trusting the Lord in my discouraged state of mind revived my hope. Call it optimism, looking on the bright side of things, or a positive state of mind. Whatever you want to call it, I knew the Lord was with me, and everything was going to be all right. I had no idea what the future looked like, didn't know how the last chapter would read, but I knew God knew, and that's all I needed to know. I'm not suggesting every day was suddenly blue skies and sunshine with songbirds singing, but I am saying I trusted Him, and He was faithful. There were days when I wanted to quit, but I trusted the Lord anyway. There were days when I wanted to get in my car and start driving and never turn back, but I trusted Him anyway. There were days when I wanted to go to sleep and not wake up, but I trusted the Lord even on those days. He was faithful to me which enabled me to be faithful to Him.

I remember many wonderful bedside conversations with elderly people who were sick and dying. They knew they had lived their life, and they were about to see what they had believed by faith. Some trembled as they spoke. Some had tears in their eyes. Some smiled. One even sang. Her name was Tess Smith. She was married to Smitty. Oh my, what good memories I have of my visits with them. I was their pastor for a few years. Mrs. Tess was sick in the bed, too frail to get up. I was visiting with her, speaking softly, reading scripture, when all of a sudden she began to move her lips quoting the scripture I was reading, John 14:1-6. I was surprised. He body was weak, but her spirit was alert. I asked her if she wanted to sing. She nodded, "yes." Together we sang the first and last verses of "Amazing Grace." She died not many days after that. She had lived her life trusting the Lord. And she died trusting the Lord.

Friend, if you're going through a difficult time and you've about given up hope that things will ever be any better, I am living proof and so is my dear friend Mrs. Tess. The Lord carried me through that difficult time of my life and has blessed me far more than I will ever deserve. I could have never predicted the goodness of God toward me. And Mrs. Tess, if she were here, would tell you not only can you trust Him while you're living, you can trust Him while you're dying. Trust the Lord and be hopeful.

BELIEVE GOD

Romans 4:3

"For what does the Scripture say? 'Abraham believed God, and it was accounted to him for righteousness.'"

You probably remember singing as a child, *"Father Abraham had many sons, many sons had Father Abraham. And I am one of them and so are you so let's just praise the Lord…"* Abraham believed God. I'm sure he also believed in God, but he did more – He believed God. I believe in the Devil, but I don't believe him. He's a liar.

Believing in God is wonderful, but to believe God is more than wonderful. It is a matter of believing what He says and what He has said. It is evidenced in doing what He says. It is evidenced in going where He sends. Believing God is far more than believing in God. It is living out what I say I believe. It is stepping out on what is visibly nothing but believing God for something. It is believing God for the evidence of things unseen. Abraham did that. And it was credited to him as righteousness.

But let's make one thing perfectly clear: It was Abraham's belief that was accounted to him for righteousness. It wasn't his works, his love for God, or any of his meaningful attributes that was accounted for righteousness. It was his belief alone, his faith alone that was credited as righteousness. Don't miss that. Because some have, and in the process have built denominations and theologies on what they presumed. The reason Abraham obeyed God was because he believed God. The reason he was willing to sacrifice his son Isaac is because he believed God. He believed God. Period. And God accounted it to him for righteousness.

When you strip away everything we do, everywhere we go, and all we say about God, we are left with what we believe about God. And when you strip down what we believe about God, what we have at the core is belief in God. Abraham believed God.

But wait a minute. Wasn't Abraham dishonest about his wife Sarah? Didn't he say she was his sister? And what about Ishmael? Didn't he get ahead of God? Abraham wouldn't get elected as a pastor in many churches today. Dishonesty and unfaithfulness seldom get a free pass. Yet for most all of his life he believed God. But what was he thinking? Why didn't he believe God at all times, especially those two times? While I can't answer for Abraham, I can answer for myself. Even as a believer I have said and done things I wish I could take back. I have failed and fallen, given up and given out, turned back and turned around, doubted and pouted more than I want to admit. Maybe Abraham was a lot like us in that he was a sinner who fell short of the glory of God. Believing God doesn't mean I am immune to temptation and sin. Maybe it means I am a sinner who believes in a God greater than my sin, bigger than my past. C. S. Lewis said, *"You can't go back and change the beginning, but you can start where you are and change the ending."* That goes for me and you and Abraham, too. Thank God for grace.

A turning point... I remember a time in my life when I was in my early twenties. I pastored a small church at that time, but I was also preaching in revival meetings whenever I could. One day I ran into a young man who had heard me preach a year or so before. As we talked, it surprised me that he remembered what I had preached. He even quoted some of what I had said in my sermon. After our conversation I sat in the car thinking about all he had remembered. I said to myself, *"People are actually listening to what I say."* It's kind of funny now, but at that point I began to realize the importance of being careful about what I preached. I remember having a conversation with myself that centered around the question, *"Did I believe what I was preaching and was I willing to build my life on it?"* I'm glad to tell you the answer was yes. I believed God. I believed and I was willing to go where He sent me. I've never looked back.

Friend, if your hope has taken a hit by hardship and disappointment, may I encourage you to believe God. When people let you down and life is hard, believe God. Regardless of what you believe in, believe Him. Believing God is a hope renewer, a hope reviver. Remind yourself of who He is. Remember His promises. Believe Him when it'd be easier to not believe.

SEEK THE LORD

Isaiah 55:6

"Seek the Lord while He may be found, Call upon Him while He is near."

Seek the Lord. What a simple admonition. I am afraid, however, that we seldom seek the Lord. We seek advice. We seek help. We seek approval. When was the last time you sought the Lord? My personal opinion is that we won't seek Him until we are at the end of ourselves, desperate for hope.

I use this verse of scripture often at the end of a sermon when I am extending an invitation to Christ. I encourage the congregation to, *"Seek the Lord while He may be found…Call upon His name while He is near."* I believe, at that time in the service, the Lord is near and can be found. I believe the power of the Gospel, the work of the Holy Spirit, and the grace of God are working, drawing the lost to be saved and the saved to be renewed. Worship is a unique time when we can hear from God. It's as if we have come in from the chaos of the world into the presence of the Lord. Suddenly, whatever is being aired on the news networks, whatever is being said in the political arena, whatever crisis is causing gas prices to rise, whatever is going on in the world, we have a refuge from it all in the presence of God. It is certainly a time to seek the Lord and call upon His name.

Our world is filled with people seeking happiness. Seeking approval. Seeking wealth. Seeking fulfillment in people, places and things. Like an old country song says, they're *"looking for love in all the wrong places."* I've been guilty of seeking to find answers outside the will of God. I've been guilty of seeking when I should have been waiting. My experience so far in this life is, at some point, most people seek the Lord, usually in a time of crisis, sickness, tragedy, or dire circumstances. Non-Christians, casual believers, and committed followers alike will seek the Lord. People who have never prayed will seek the Lord when their back is against the wall and their world is on fire. I know a few folks who became believers after being backed into a corner by life's difficulties. When you're on a stretcher or in an emergency room, your perspective changes. Your death or that of someone you love becomes a reality. I encourage you today, friend, if there's never been a time when you sought the Lord, seek Him now before the crisis. While you're able to think rationally. Seek Him now, and when the crisis comes you'll already know His peace and presence.

If Arvid Wakefield could speak, I think he'd agree with me. Before Dawn was my wife, she was married to Arvid, who died after an extended battle with ALS. Arvid and I became friends when I was in my early twenties and remained close until his death. Arvid's diagnosis was a shock to him and Dawn. But they were already believers, and even though they were heartbroken with the news, they didn't lose faith. If anything, their faith increased during the illness. Arvid's faith in God during that time became a beacon of hope to anyone struggling with a life crisis. At one of my visits with him he told me how he thanked the Lord for ALS because it had brought him closer to the Lord than he had ever been in his life.

What does Arvid's sickness have to do with *"seeking the Lord while He may be found?"* Ask any believer who has been diagnosed with a life-threatening illness. They will tell you that God is real in the storm. More real than before the storm. It's not that Arvid's illness made his and Dawn's faith strong; it only revealed how strong it already was. They sought the Lord in a difficult season of uncertainty. They sought God as believers praying for a miracle. While the miracle of healing didn't happen on this side of Heaven, Dawn will tell you countless stories of grace that did happen. She will also tell you of all the "even-ifs" that God carried them through. Even if the diagnosis is not what we wanted... Even if he loses the ability to care for himself... Even if he goes to Heaven before the rest of us... God is enough. More than enough. And that is reason enough to seek Him.

What about you? Maybe you've lost a loved one recently. Maybe you have a friend who's battling sickness and the outlook seems hopeless. Don't you believe it. "Hopeless" shouldn't be a part of the believer's vocabulary. We have hope when we have nothing else. But, if for some reason you are without hope today, seek the Lord. Call on His name. Bear your heart and soul to God. Cry out to God. When you seek Him you will find Him. When you call on Him, He is near.

Maybe it's because I am older now, but I have learned to seek the Lord first. When I was younger I sought advice, opinions, direction, etc. And much of what I sought was good. But there is no substitute for the counsel of the Lord. Whatever decision you are facing, seek the Lord and call on His name. Whatever difficulty, seek the Lord and call on His name. Whether you're in the valley or on the mountaintop, seek Him. One day you'll look back, and you'll be glad you did.

ABIDE IN HIM

John 15:5

"I am the vine, you are the branches. He who abides in Me, and I in him, bears much fruit; for without Me you can do nothing."

At the beginning of each year Dawn chooses a "word for the year." A word that defines where she is in life or where she wants to be. I mentioned to her I was writing a devotional about abiding in Christ. She immediately said, *"That was my word in 2015."* I'm including her thoughts, along with mine, as I encourage you to abide in Him.

Dawn wrote in her blog back in 2015, which was the year following her late husband's passing, *"The reason I chose "abide" to be my word for 2015 is because the past few years of my life has been anything but calm." I could not use words like peaceful, restful, tranquil, or serene."* After Arvid's diagnosis back in 2010, he along with Dawn and their family traveled a winding road filled with hope, disappointment, and abiding. Maybe someone reading this can relate. No two stories are the same, but most folks have a story of hope and disappointment. Dawn's story is different from many because it includes abiding in Christ through all the highs and lows. I must add, I'm not suggesting that "abiding in Christ" is always easy or that the ride is always smooth. Personally, I have had to grit my teeth at times because I wanted to take matters into my own hands. But to release the situation into God's hands is amazingly peaceful.

Abiding is a daily commitment. Abiding is a daily calling. In her blog Dawn wrote, *"When I began to dig a little deeper into the meaning of abide, I felt a calm in my soul. I felt comfort there."* She continued with a beautiful description of a place that is *"protected, safe, unrushed, restored."* Yes…yes…yes. Maybe you've been there. Abiding in Him won't allow you to be bitter, angry, or resentful. Those feelings may cross your mind, but you can't dwell there because you're content in Him. Abiding is a hopeful place to be. Depending on God's sufficiency rather than trusting in your own strength restores and rebuilds all that you may have lost through fear and anxiety.

Dawn wrote, *"The word "abide" is not about 'doing' but 'being.'"* Abiding means I resist the temptation to do something in response to what has been done to me. It means to "be" instead of "do." Be still. Be patient. Be wise. Be content. And sometimes I think it means to be quiet and listen to God. God is always speaking if we can only get in position to hear Him. There'll be days when only what you hear from God will help you. Encouragement from friends is nice, but a word from God is life changing.

Back in 2015 Dawn described ALS as an enemy that had invaded their home. She wrote about a battle with that enemy and how it changed their family forever. She said, *"I am weary from this battle. I am lonely after this battle. There are now pieces of me that are missing. But as I write these words I know that the victory is ours, and I know it is because of the One I call Savior....As I abide in Him, He will be the source from which my healing comes. "* Abiding in Him is the source of our healing and hope.

Guard your heart from anything that tries to pull you away from abiding in Him. Beware of worry. Be on guard for resentment. Be watchful for fear and doubt. Abide in him like a branch abides in the vine. Attach yourself to Him, and don't allow anything to pull you away. The branch can do nothing unless it abides in the vine. And we find our hope in Him.

It's been over five years since Dawn wrote about abiding in Christ. Those were more than mere words she wrote back then. What she wrote was more than a good idea or good intentions. She has lived what she wrote. She is abiding in Him still today. I want you to know, friend, that this God we serve is real! He really does bring beauty from ashes. He actually does work all things together for our good. His grace is certainly all sufficient. He is real. You can abide in him. He is our Hope.

AFTERWORD

I trust this brief volume has helped and encouraged you. When I was a pastor, seldom did a week pass that someone didn't drop by to see me and say, *"I just need to talk to you a few minutes."* Often that *"few minutes"* became an hour or more. I usually asked, *"How can I help you?"* The truth is they were not looking for help. They were looking for hope. Over time I have learned to agree with John Maxwell when he said, *"Most folks aren't looking to understand, they just want to be understood."* They're hurting, and they need someone to care.

Vance Havner said, *"You may not be able to trace the hand of God, but you can always trust the heart of God."* That hits home with most of us. We'd like to know why and how and when. We'd like to know the details, to be able to discern the times, and to be able to predict the future. Peace of mind won't be found in reading your horoscope or paying the lady at the carnival to read your palm. Peace comes only in trusting the heart of God.

My friend, Junior Hill, says there are times when you have to stand even when you don't understand. Can you relate to that?

You have to believe God is with you even when there is no evidence. You have to believe He is holding your hand even when you can't feel His grip. You have to believe He is lighting your path even when there seems to be darkness all around. Standing when you don't understand is one of the most difficult things you'll ever do. But the reward is sweet. What is the reward? Remember the footprints in the sand? For a time there were two sets of prints in the sand. God was walking with you. Then when trouble came there was only one set of prints. Why? It was during the troubled times God was carrying you. The sweetness of the reward is a result of your faithfulness in difficult times.

Ruth Graham, the wife of the great evangelist Billy Graham, went home to Heaven in June of 2007. Billy was interviewed by TIME magazine later that same year. His love for Ruth was evident for all their life together. But in that article he let the world know that the best was yet to come. He said, *"Heaven is where Ruth is. Someday soon I will join her. Most of all I take comfort in the hope we can have of eternal life in Heaven because of Christ's death and resurrection for us. I've preached this message almost all my life, and it means more to me now than ever before."*

Billy Graham's hope was in Christ alone. When it's all said and done, our faith is about so much more than the churches we attend, sermons we preach, and the songs we sing. When we have nothing left at all—when we've lost our health and the doctors say all hope is gone—it's not. Believers in Christ may lose their life, but they never lose their hope.

I have been saved almost forty years. I have been disappointed, worried, heartbroken, upset, and fearful. But I have never been hopeless. During the darkest season of my life there were times when I felt lonely, but I never felt alone. I may leave this world sick or poor or unpopular, but I won't leave here without hope. I would like to be like Billy Graham...live and preach into my nineties. But if life ended today, I am blessed. All because of Christ. He is my Hope.

ABOUT THE AUTHOR

Michael Mason is the President of Michael Mason Ministries, Inc. Having served as a vocational evangelist (traveling preacher) for over 25 years, and pastoring for thirteen years, he remains busy speaking at numerous conferences, revivals, and other evangelistic services.

He is a graduate of Athens State University, New Orleans Baptist Theological Seminary, and The Southern BaptistTheological Seminary.

He is married to Dawn. Together they have five children and four grandchildren. They reside in Hartselle, Alabama.

He is the author of two other books: *Deep Dark Holes*, and *Faithful*.

For booking information and for copies of his books visit michaelmasonministries.com or email Michael at michael-mason@charter.net.

Made in the USA
Columbia, SC
14 July 2021